Ideas for Junior High Leaders

Ideas for Junior High Leaders: A Junior High Program Planner

by

Matilda Nordtvedt

and

Pearl Steinkuehler

MOODY PRESS

CHICAGO

Contents

1
Mission Impossible?

I am an iceberg and only one-fourth of me
    is shown to others.
Only one-fourth of me is above the surface of the
    impenetrable waters that conceal my inner self . . .
    the real me.
Does anyone dare . . .
To search beneath those waters . . .
Does anyone dare . . .
To understand me?[1]

Will we dare to try to understand the fourteen-year-old who wrote those pleading words? Will we try to see her as a person struggling to find out who she is and why she exists?

Teacher, how well do you know your junior highers? Do you describe them as "impossible"? Have you a Kevin, a John, a Sherrie, a roomful of Nans and Karris, and even a Rod or two?

Kevin had never been to youth group before. John

1. From *Understanding Youth,* by T. Garvice and Dorothy Murphree, © 1969, Convention Press, Nashville. All rights reserved. Used by permission.

brought him along. When Kevin's language and actions went from bad to worse, John muttered to the perplexed teacher, "I knew I never should have brought him to church."

Sherrie seems to know the answers, and she wants to participate in discussions, but she turns beet-red every time anyone looks at her and can scarcely stammer out a word.

Mark speaks up occasionally, but when his voice switches from bass to tenor he looks embarrassed and sometimes angry at the giggles that follow his voice switcheroo.

Rob can't walk, sit, or stand up without tripping over something, often his own oversized feet dangling from super-long, spindly legs. Tiny is equally "graceful" in her growth spurt.

Jim challenges everyone to arm wrestle—even while you're trying to teach a Bible lesson. His brain may be lazy, but his biceps bulge nicely.

Jolene sits quietly in class. Her vacant stare and Mona Lisa smile suggest that her mind is vacationing in Hawaii.

Suzy is bouncy and bubbly one moment, the life of the party. Seconds later, she bursts into tears and runs from the room. *Who knows what brought that on?* we all wonder.

Karri thinks she is one big "zit." Matt appears to have visited the same chocolate factory, but Karri seems unaware she has lots of company in "Zitsville." She says she'll "just die" if her face doesn't clear up before Marti's big party.

Nan is in love. The world knows it. She has doodled Rob's name on her bulletin, her quarterly, the table, and even her hand!

Everyone tries to get to the goodies before Bret does. They call him "bottomless pit," but they're no slouches at the table, either.

Charlotte talks to you a lot and even volunteers to do projects. Kathy and Judy call her a teacher's pet. They walk away whenever she approaches.

Eric literally waddles into class. Julie could model for

Mr. Lewis's science class skeleton—a likely candidate for anorexia nervosa.

Bill nods through whatever is going on. An occasional snore escapes him. Joe pokes him, and the group roars in laughter.

Rod is high one moment, dull the next. Rumors say he visits "Smoker's Alley" after school to smoke grass.

What's that the kids quit talking about when you came in? Did you hear "chicken, beer bust, everyone's going" before they shushed each other and put on churchy expressions?

You may think you are the only teacher with such impossible kids. Unfortunately, this kind of behavior is typical of this age group—no longer children, but not yet adults.

Yours is a group of becomers—good one moment, rebellious the next—very unpredictable. You have the task and privilege of helping them to become the best they can be under God. Yours is the task of leading them to acknowledge with Paul that he had not yet attained, but also encouraging them to "press on toward the goal for the prize of the upward call of God in Jesus Christ" (Philippians 3:13-14).

An old expression says, "When the going gets tough, the tough get going." When a situation is "impossible," the good teacher prays more and tries harder. We, the authors, hope this book will help you in your "going."

2
Mission Control

Junior highers can be extremely difficult. Probably no group in the church is so hard to manage. Many junior high leaders throw up their hands in despair. Their students are unresponsive, bored, critical of one another, disruptive, and impossible.

If your junior highers act that way, they are probably only following a ringleader or two. If you can win the ringleaders to your side, you will be able to control the whole group.

First of all, try to get to know the troublemakers. What kind of homes do they come from? They may come from large families, in which parents are too busy to give them much attention. Or they may come from broken homes and feel rejected by one or both parents.

That means you must make an effort to give that junior higher special attention. If your troublemaker is a boy, try taking him fishing with you or go out for pizza together some evening. If one of your junior high girls is the disrupter, invite her over to help you make cookies or to plan a special junior high event.

Another factor to consider is the youth's self-image. If you are sensitive to the one who creates a disturbance,

you will most likely discover that he has extremely low
self-esteem. He feels that the only way he can be recog-
nized is to make a nuisance out of himself.

There are ways to improve a person's self-esteem.
Besides giving him special attention, you can find jobs for
him to do, for which you praise him privately. Public
praise would embarrass him and create other problems.
Giving him some responsibility will boost his self-esteem.
When he feels good about himself he won't be so likely to
misbehave.

Sometimes a leader resorts to anger to gain control.
That may seem effective for a short while, but it is not a
lasting solution. Firmness, yes; anger, no. If you become
angry with the offender, he will feel even more rejected
than he did before, and the situation will be aggravated
rather than improved.

Inform the young people that it is their *privilege* to
come to the youth group. Set up, with the class, some
ground rules for behavior. You may choose to allow talking during the first few minutes of the meeting, but when
the class begins expect full attention. One person speaking at a time, giving each a turn to speak, is a good rule
to follow. The speaker has the right to be listened to by
all the others.

If the group gets noisy, don't try to outyell them. Just
stop talking. They will quiet down and return their attention to you. And if you must discipline a junior higher, do
it in private. Scorn, sarcasm, and public embarrassment
are never appropriate for Christians.

It might be helpful to recruit other adults to help you on
a rotating basis. Select the parents of some of your youth
to serve as "Mom and Dad" for a month or a quarter. Use
them as group leaders, craft or game resource persons,
and chaperones. They could privately work with teens
who would then lead games or other activities at youth
group.

Don't forget to pray. God works wonders through
believing prayer, even in impossible junior highers. Bring
your misbehavers to Him often and trust Him to work.
You'll find that He will give you patience and understand-

ing when you wait before Him in prayer. He will also work in the hearts of the youth you are trying to help.

If you work with junior highers, a sense of humor is a must. Keep the atmosphere light and happy, even as you teach the momentous truths of the Bible. Learn to good-naturedly overlook some of their harmless antics.

Keep them so busy that they won't have time to misbehave. Don't make the mistake of coming to your group unprepared, expecting them to take the lead. Know what you are going to do beforehand. Have a plan. Let the youth make suggestions and plans, but always be ready with a plan of your own. Being caught with nothing to do, or only a vague idea, will result in disaster: boredom and disruptive behavior. You'll find your junior highers dropping out unless you have something interesting and challenging planned for each time you meet.

It doesn't have to be all "fun and games." Junior highers are concerned about serious matters, too. They want to know how they can be acceptable to God, get along with their parents, and do something worthwhile with their lives. They'll soon become dissatisfied if you do not feed them from God's Word. Lead them to see how Bible truths apply to their lives today.

But, of course, their times together must also be fun. Competition, sharing time, games, projects, and responsibility must all be a part of a balanced youth program. Physical activity uses up energy that could lead to disruptive behavior.

Above all, show them that you care about them as individuals. They know whether you love them or not. Keeping a notebook with a page for each young person is helpful. Write down his birthday, likes, dislikes, hobbies, what he wants to be when he grows up, home situation, problems, and spiritual progress. Johnny will be pleased that you remember he wants to be an astronaut someday.

Ask an adult what he remembers most about his own youth leader. Nine times out of ten he will think a moment and then say, "He/she really loved me."

Understanding each youth, giving him something vital from the Word, being patient but firm, having a sense of humor, preparing fun activities, and loving—those are the essentials, "but the greatest of these is love" (1 Corinthians 13:13).

3
Message Plus Methods

Try on these messages and teaching methods for size. We think they will fit your junior highers.

What Difference Does the Bible Make?

The longest chapter in the Bible is Psalm 119. It is a discussion about God's Word. The psalmist calls God's Word His law, precepts, testimonies, ordinances, statutes, commandments, and judgments.

Divide your group into two sides by counting off by twos. Have a contest to explore Psalm 119. Find out what God's Word is and what it does for the psalmist and for us.

Each side must plan its own strategy, such as dividing up the psalm among its members so each person doesn't have to read it all. Have each team assign a captain to write down the answers as the searchers find them. Be sure they also write down the numbers of the verses where their answers are found.

List answers in two columns:

What God's Word Is: What God's Word Does:

The side that finds the most answers, in a given period

of time, wins. Write the words for God's Word on the chalkboard: word, statutes, testimonies, law, commandments, precept, ordinances, judgments, and others. Also write an example:

<table>
<tr><td>What God's Word Is:
a lamp unto my feet
   (v. 105)</td><td>What God's Word Does:
keeps a young man pure
   (v. 9)</td></tr>
</table>

Ready, set, go—
Here is a possible list. Theirs may not be as long.

What God's Word Is:	**What God's Word Does:**
my delight (v. 24)	keeps a young man pure (v. 8)
my counselors (v. 24)	keeps a person from sin (v. 11)
good (v. 39)	gives me liberty (v. 45)
my song (v. 54)	revives me (v. 50)
better than thousands of gold and silver pieces (v. 72)	teaches me (v. 66)
righteous (v. 75)	makes me wiser than my enemies (v. 98)
faithful (v. 86)	gives me more insight than my teachers (v. 99)
settled in heaven (v. 89)	gives me more understanding than the aged (v. 100)
exceedingly broad (v. 96)	restrains my feet from evil (v. 101)
my meditation (v. 97)	gives light (v. 130)
sweeter than honey (v. 103)	gives peace (v. 165)
lamp to my feet (v. 105)	keeps me from stumbling (v. 165)
light to my path (v. 105)	
the joy of my heart (v. 111)	
wonderful (v. 129)	
very pure (v. 140)	
truth (v. 151)	
everlasting (v. 160)	

If enthusiasm continues, try this one. Have the teams write down all the sentences in Psalm 119 that show the psalmist's attitude toward God's Word. See which side wins this time.

Attitude of Psalmist to God's Word

I have treasured Thy word in my heart (v. 11).
I have rejoiced in the way of Thy testimonies (v. 64).
I observe Thy testimonies (v. 22).
I meditate on Thy statutes (v. 23).
I have placed Thine ordinances before me (v. 30).
I cleave to Thy testimonies (v. 31).
I long for Thy precepts (v. 40).
I trust in Thy Word (v. 42).
I wait for Thine ordinances (v. 43).
I will keep Thy law continually (v. 44).
I seek Thy precepts (v. 45).
I will speak of Thy testimonies (v. 46).
I do not turn aside from Thy law (v. 51).
I have remembered Thine ordinances (v. 52).
I have promised to keep Thy words (v. 57).
I believe in Thy commandments (v. 66).
I delight in Thy law (v. 70).
I love Thy law (v. 97).
I have inherited Thy testimonies forever (v. 111).
I love Thy commandments above gold (v. 127).
My heart stands in awe of Thy words (v. 161).
I rejoice at Thy word as one who finds great spoil (v. 162).
I do not forget Thy commandments (v. 176).

Summarize their findings briefly, showing them what God's Word can do for them: give light, guide, keep from sin, give understanding, and give peace.

Discuss the difficulties of reading God's Word: hard words, little time, and so on. Encourage the young people to read a modern version a few minutes a day, starting with Matthew and reading through the New Testament. Tell them to write down in a notebook one thing they learn each day—a command to obey, a promise to trust, or a sin to confess. Give them an opportunity to share their findings at a later meeting.

Add to this lesson on a Hebrew psalm by learning these songs: "Books of the Old Testament" and "Books of the New Testament." They will aid in any Scripture search. Sung to the tune of "Have You Ever Seen a Lassie?" the words may be found in children's chorus books.

Does Prayer Really Work?

Before class: Enlist a youth or two to begin preparing a bulletin board in the room. Put on the board cut-out letters that read, "God Answers Prayer. . . ." Cut out three large outlines of praying hands: one yellow, one brown, and one white. Write Group One questions on the yellow hands, Group Two on the brown hands, and Group Three on the white ones.

Ask the young people to share answers to prayers they have had. Share some of your own: small problems, such as finding a book you needed; large answers, such as the salvation of a loved one or the physical healing of a friend; and personal answers, such as God's meeting you with a promise from His Book when you were feeling lonely, afraid, or depressed.

Divide into three groups. Give each group a praying hands cutout and a marker. Have the young people answer their questions. Instruct the secretary of each group to write on the blank side of the hands their key word: "yes," "no," or "wait."

Group One:

1. Why does God not answer our prayers (Psalm 66:18; Isaiah 59:1-2)?
   Answer: Because of unconfessed sin in our lives.
2. Give another reason God does not answer our prayers (James 4:3).
   Answer: We pray with wrong motives and selfish reasons.
3. Give an example of a "yes" answer from James 5:17.
   Answer: God withheld rain in answer to Elijah's prayer.

Group Two:

1. Give an example of God's saying no to a prayer from
   2 Corinthians 12:7-9. Why do you think He said no?
   Answer: Paul asked for his thorn to be removed—
   maybe a sickness; some think an eye disease. God
   did not heal Paul. He wanted Paul to learn to depend
   on Him, to trust Him, to experience His power in his
   weakness.
2. Joni Eareckson broke her neck in a diving accident
   and is paralyzed from her neck down. She prayed for
   healing, but God did not heal her. Why did He say
   no?
   Answer: God wants to show His power through Joni.
   She is happy in spite of living in a wheelchair and
   shows multitudes that God is real.

Group Three:

1. Read John 11:1-6, 17, 38-45. Mary and Martha sent
   for Jesus to come and heal their brother, Lazarus.
   Jesus, upon getting the message, stayed two days
   longer where He was. Meanwhile, Lazarus died. What
   was Jesus saying to their prayer?
   Answer: Wait.
2. As you read the rest of the story you will see that
   Jesus raised Lazarus from the dead. Why do you
   think Jesus said, "Wait"?
   Answer: He wanted to do something even greater for
   them. He wanted to show His power to many people
   so they would believe.
3. Why would He say, "Wait," to your prayers
   sometimes?
   Answer: He has a better plan.

Bring the groups together and discuss their findings. Be
sure to remind the young people that sometimes we do
not understand what God is doing but must simply trust
His love and wisdom. Ask the group leaders to finish the
bulletin board by placing the "yes," "no," and "wait"

sides of the hands to complete the phrase "God Answers Prayer. . . ."

Assemble in groups again and have each group make up a short skit to illustrate their point. You may have to give a suggestion or two to get them started.

Group One:

A girl prays for a job so she can get money to buy cigarettes or drugs.

A boy prays for help on a test for which he studied hard.

A girl prays she'll beat her tennis rival because she doesn't like her.

Group Two:

A brother and sister pray their dad won't be transferred, because they don't want to move to another town. God says no. They move and find neat Christian friends in their new town, as well as opportunities to serve God. They realize God knew what was best for them.

Group Three:

A boy prays for his father to stop drinking. God says, "Wait." The boy learns patience by waiting, and his faith is strengthened. Eventually his dad not only stops drinking, but he also becomes a Christian.

Give each junior higher a small notebook. Encourage them to write down their prayer requests in their little books, marking down the date when they begin to pray about something and the date when that prayer is answered. Begin developing the prayer list habit by having them list at least one prayer request at this time. Ask them to watch for answers to prayer and to be prepared for times when God answers their prayers differently than what they expected.

Pros and Cons of Being a Christian

Hand out slips of paper and pencils. Have the young people list the pros and cons of being a Christian. Explain the words *pro* and *con,* if they don't understand them.

After they have worked for a few minutes, write their conclusions on the chalkboard or an overhead projector transparency under the two headings. Add your own convictions to theirs.

PRO	CON
No guilty conscience	It's hard to be different
Sins are forgiven—peace	Have to go a different direction than everyone else
Reason for living	It's hard to do what's right
Jesus always with me	There are some things Christians can't do, like take drugs
I have Someone who understands me	Might miss out on some fun
I have Someone who looks out for me	Can't go all the places my friends go
Help in time of need	Might be left out of the "in" group
All things work together for good	Might be made fun of
Guidance in my decisions	Might lose friends
Lasting joy instead of temporary joy	Have to stand alone
Hope for now and the future	Might be lonely sometimes
Everlasting life	
Know for sure where I'm going—heaven	
Future reward	
Privilege of reigning with Christ	

After discussing the pros and cons, ask your young people to feel under their chairs and find the strips of paper you taped there before class. Each strip will list one of the following Scripture references. Each person will look up his verse and read it to the group. If your group is small, write two or more references on each strip.

Psalm 16:11	Romans 5:1
Psalm 32:8	Romans 8:1
Psalm 73:23	Romans 8:18
Psalm 73:24	Romans 8:28
Psalm 103:12	Romans 15:13
Psalm 121:2	2 Timothy 4:8
Psalm 139:1	Hebrews 13:5
Matthew 28:20	1 John 5:13
John 3:16	Revelation 3:21

Talk about the wisdom of denying oneself immediate pleasure for long term profit. Emphasize that Christians have more fun than anyone, because they don't have to feel guilty after their fun. Their joy doesn't depend on what happens to them—they know God is leading them, and underneath it all they have an eternal hope that brightens everything.

Invite any young people who have never accepted Christ and would like to receive Him to talk to you privately after your session.

Variation: Make lists of what you gain and what you lose when you become a Christian (gain peace, hope, and heaven; lose guilt, fear, and dread of future).

Attitude of Gratitude

Read or have two students read the following conversation:

Pete: I was riding in an airplane the other day.
Zeke: That's good.
Pete: But we ran out of gas.
Zeke: Oh, that's bad.
Pete: But I had a parachute.
Zeke: Oh, that's good.
Pete: But the parachute didn't open.
Zeke: Oh, that's bad!
Pete: But there was a haystack under me.
Zeke: That's good!
Pete: But there was a pitchfork in the haystack.
Zeke: Oh, that's bad!
Pete: But I missed the pitchfork!

(Zeke faints)

Can you find something good in what happens to you, as Pete did? What does the Bible say? Pass out slips of paper with the following Scripture references. Have your junior highers work in pairs, looking up the verses and summarizing what they find about thankfulness.

1. Romans 8:28—All things work together for good for Christians.
2. Psalm 9:1—I should thank Him with my whole heart.
3. Psalm 34:1—I should thank Him at all times.
4. Hebrews 13:15—I should praise Him continually.
5. Ephesians 5:20—I should give thanks for all things.
6. 1 Thessalonians 5:18—I should give thanks in every-thing (in every situation).
7. Colossians 2:7—I should overflow with gratitude.

Come together and write the findings on the board. Then form pairs again. Each pair shouid choose a calamity or difficulty of some kind and write out a dialogue like the one at the beginning about the parachute, showing how the calamity works together for good so we should be thankful for it. For instance:

Jeff: I broke my leg yesterday.
Mutt: That's bad.
Jeff: But I didn't have to go to school.
Mutt: That's good.
Jeff: But I had to make up my algebra test.
Mutt: That's bad.
Jeff: But I had lots of time to study.
Mutt: That's good.
Jeff: But I studied the wrong lesson.
Mutt: That's bad.
Jeff: But the teacher felt sorry for me and gave me an "A," anyway.
(Mutt faints)

The dialogues may be humorous, or even ridiculous. After each pair has given theirs, seriously discuss how God makes broken legs, accidents, sickness, disappoint-

ments, and losses work together for our good. Talk about
the benefits Christians derive from hardships and even
calamities: closeness to God, trust, patience, true values,
character, wisdom, maturity, and understanding of
others.

Talk about having an attitude of gratitude, even for the
difficult things that come to our lives. Review the points
on thankfulness: we are to overflow with gratitude—to
give thanks with all our hearts, at all times, continually,
for all things, in every circumstance. Talk about how this
attitude of gratitude not only pleases God and makes us a
testimony to others, but also makes us happy people.
Have short prayers of thanks for the unpleasant as well
as the pleasant things God allows to come to us.

Christmas Is Giving

Tell the youth group the true story of the high school
girl and boy in Minnesota who decided that, instead of
giving Christmas presents to each other, they would use
the money to give a happy Christmas to someone less for-
tunate than themselves. Choosing a little retarded boy in
a children's home, they bought him a truck, took him
sledding, and then treated him to a hamburger and a bas-
ketball game. The little boy loved it, and they had a wonderful time, too.

Look up Matthew 25:40 and talk about it. When we do
something kind for others because we love the Lord, He
says it is the same as doing it for Him.

Discuss how you could give the Lord a birthday present
He would really be pleased with by doing something kind
for someone in need. Consider these ideas.

1. Make Christmas Goodie Candles to pass out at a local
   nursing home or distribute to other shut-ins you
   know (see directions in chapter 8). Fill the candles
   with cookies and candies, making some with artificial
   sweeteners that are safe for diabetics.
2. Bring a gift to a young person in the hospital. If he
   will be there for some time give him a "made with

love'' twelve days of Christmas box (see directions in chapter 8).
3. Go caroling at a rest home.
4. Instead of exchanging gifts, each bring a gift for a refugee child or some other person in need. Wrap them in Christmas paper together after you have enjoyed comparing gifts. Include a Bible, if the person does not have one.

Is Anybody Hungry?

On enough slips of paper for all but two of your young people write: "Resident of Third World Country." On one slip write, "American." On another write, "American brought up in a Christian home." Fold the slips, put them in a pretty bowl, and pass it, letting each junior higher draw out a slip.

Put the two who picked "American" and "American brought up in a Christian home" by themselves at a small table. Bring them two large pizzas. (The others will no doubt protest.) Explain that this is what is happening in our world. People in privileged countries like America have plenty to eat—and even too much—while people in third-world countries, like India, are starving.

Place an open Bible beside the person who drew "American brought up in a Christian home." Place a closed Bible within reach of the one who drew "American." Explain that kids brought up in Christian homes have a spiritual feast—they learn about God and the Bible from the time they are small. The other American has a chance to find out about God and His Word if he wants to, because Bibles and churches are available where he lives. Most residents of third-world countries are not only starving for physical food, but also for spiritual food, the Word of God, which can show them the way to everlasting life.

Ask the two privileged ones with the pizzas and the Bibles what they are going to do with what they have. No doubt they will agree to share their pizza with the others. Encourage them to do so. As you all munch on pizza, talk about the responsibility of Americans to share food with

starving people and the responsibility of Christians to
share the Word with those who have never heard.

Plan ways together to share both temporal and spiritual
blessings. Be practical. A junior higher can't give a large
donation to world relief, but he can bring a food item each
week to give to the Salvation Army or some other organi-
zation feeding the hungry in your city. Your group can
plan ways to raise money to give to world relief organizations and mission organizations that are spreading the
Word. Remind them that, although they must be concerned about the physical needs of people, they must be
equally or even more concerned about their spiritual eternal welfare.

Lead them to suggest ways to share what they have
with the needy of the world. How about making banks
out of pop cans for their spare change? (Look at chapter 4
for ideas on service projects.)

Share these statistics:

There are thirty countries in the world that have a per
capita income of less than $100.

There are 450 million malnourished people in the world
(1 out of every 10).

In Africa's Sahel region, 70 percent of the people do not
receive enough food to eat.

In 1980 in Djibouti, a tiny country on the horn of
Africa, children were given only one drink of water a day;
adults drank every other day.

About 2000 different language groups have no Bible as
yet.

Ninety percent of all Christian workers work with 10 percent of the world's population, leaving 90 percent of the
world's population with 10 percent of the Christian workers. (To update statistics write to: World Concern, Box
33000, Seattle, WA 98133.)

New Year's Musings

Before class time, enlist a couple of young people to
help you prepare scroll-like sheets of paper in five different pastel shades, making one for each youth expected.
Singe the lower edge of each scroll, then roll and tie it.

These helpers may give one to each youth as he enters the classroom, alternating colors so that closest friends won't receive the same color.

Don't tell the young people what the scrolls are for until goal-setting time, but use the colors of their scrolls to divide them into five study groups.

Assign each group one of the following topics as related to the new year they have just entered.

1. I Look Not Back—Discuss why we shouldn't look back on our failures (read Isaiah 43:25; Micah 7:19; 1 John 1:9).
2. I Look Not Forward—Discuss the mistake of living in the future and being anxious about what is going to happen (read Proverbs 3:5-6; Jeremiah 29:11; Matthew 28:20; Philippians 4:6-7).
3. I Look Not Around Me—Discuss being troubled by current events, trends, tragedies, and wars (read Isaiah 41:10,13; 43:1-2; Hebrews 3:5-6).
4. I Look Not in Me—Discuss looking at self and worrying about one's standing before God (read Romans 5:1; 8:1, 33-34).
5. I Look to Jesus—Discuss the "upward look" to the Lord for forgiveness of sins and failures, hope for the future, strength for today, right standing before God (read Psalm 123:1-2; Isaiah 17:7; 45:22; Hebrews 12:2).

Come together and discuss findings. Learn an appropriate song.

After establishing the focus for the new year, talk about goals. Ask each person to unroll his scroll and write down his personal goals for the new year. Some may be willing to share their goals with the others.

Set class goals as a group. Write these on the chalkboard and on a sheet of paper. Ask an artistic youth to chart the goals on poster board to hang on the wall to keep the plans before the young people. Since you're trying to get them to look up, post the list on the ceiling for a week or two. When the novelty wears off, put it in a less neck-cricking spot.

Some suggestions for class goals:
1. Raise $100 for the hungry.
2. Put on two programs for the church.
3. Try to double the number of the youth group (each one bring a new person).
4. Do an outdoor cleaning at the church in the spring.
5. Memorize a Bible verse every week.

Dating and Marriage

Before the meeting: Cut out equal numbers of construction paper hearts, roses, and rings, making enough for each youth to have one cutout. Arrange chairs in a circle and place a cutout on each chair, alternating them so that no two like symbols are on adjoining chairs.

After the young people are all seated, say, "In many cultures of our world, dating as we know it is not practiced. Parents arrange marriages for their children. Sometimes a couple does not meet until shortly before the wedding. In our culture, however, young people date. There are two reasons for dating: to have fun and companionship with the opposite sex and to prepare for marriage. What does the Bible have to say about this important subject?"

Divide your junior highers into three groups for buzz sessions. Tell them to pick up their chairs and form circles in three areas of the room. Those with hearts will be Group 1; roses, Group 2; and rings, Group 3. Give each group one of the sets of questions to work out together. Provide paper and pens for the "secretary" of each group to record the findings. Each group will choose one member to report their findings to the rest of the groups when they reassemble.

Group One

1. Who invented marriage (Genesis 2:20-24)?
   Answer: God
2. What does God say about sex outside of marriage (Hebrews 13:4)?
   Answer: It will be judged.
3. Why is it important for Christians to date other Chris-

tians, instead of unbelievers (2 Corinthians 6:14)?
List as many reasons as you can.
Answer: Christians may be influenced away from God
if they date unbelievers. They may fall in love and
want to marry.

4. What happened to the world when godly people
   started to intermarry with the ungodly (Genesis 6:2,
   5-6, 12)?
   Answer: The godly became wicked; people turned
   away from God.

Group Two

1. Trace King Solomon's fall into sin and idolatry. What
   started it (1 Kings 11:1-10)?
   Answer: His marriage to a heathen woman. He mar-
   ried more and more heathen women. Trying to please
   them, he ended up in idolatry himself.
2. What does 2 Corinthians 6:14 say about this?
   Answer: We are not to be united with unbelievers.

Group Three

1. What big mistake did the godly King Jehoshaphat
   make (2 Chronicles 18:1)?
   Answer: Arranged for his son to marry the daughter
   of wicked King Ahab of Israel.
2. Discover how this mistake affected his children,
   grandchildren, and many other people (2 Chronicles
   21:5-6; 22:2-3, 10-11).
   Answer: Athaliah, the ungodly wife, introduced idolatry, led her family away from God, killed her own
   grandchildren in order to reign herself, and led the
   people of Judah into idolatry and evil.

Bring groups together to report findings and discuss
modern-day parallels to the Bible accounts. Use illustra-
tions from your own circle of acquaintances. You probably know or have heard of the following:

1. A Christian fellow dates an unbeliever, falls in love
   with her, and decides to marry her. She gradually
   influences him to stop going to church.

2. A Christian girl dates the wrong kind of boy. She gets
   pregnant and marries him to give her child a father.
   They are too young and have nothing in common.
   The marriage ends in divorce.
3. A Christian fellow dates an unbelieving girl and
   starts running with her crowd.
4. The children of unequally yoked parents become con-
   fused as to which parent to follow. They may follow
   the non-Christian instead of the Christian.

Play an active game as a group to relax tensions discussing this subject might have brought on. Select a few
who enjoy cooking to make pizzas while most play the
game. Suggest they form the pizza crusts into shapes:
hearts, flowers, circles, butterflies, any shape they wish.
Let the players pick the most unique pizza. Recognize the
creative chef as "The Future Homemaker of America."

What About Moods?

A Campa woman of Peru expresses her mood by paint-
ing a design on her face. An arrow means she's in a good
mood and would like to talk to those around her. But if
she has painted a scorpion on her face, watch out! That
means she's in a very bad mood and will strike out at
anyone who doesn't leave her alone!

We don't paint scorpions on our faces, but we express
our moods in other ways: by anger, depression, or
pouting.

Divide into three groups according to birthday months.
Assign each group a character from the Bible to study
and report back to the others for discussion. Those born
in January through April are Ahab; May through August,
Elijah; September through December, Jonah.

King Ahab—1 Kings 21:1-4

1. What brought on Ahab's bad mood?
   Answer: He didn't get what he wanted.
2. How did he react?
   Answer: He went to bed and pouted.

3. How might a teenager act when he doesn't get his way?

Elijah—1 Kings 18:46—19:7

1. What brought on Elijah's bad mood?
   Answer: He became too tired.
2. How did he react?
   Answer: He became depressed, gave up, and wanted to die.
3. What did he need?
   Answer: Rest and food.
4. Could a teenager become depressed from the same cause?

Jonah—Jonah 3:10—4:1-11

1. What brought on Jonah's bad mood?
   Answer: God spared Nineveh—things didn't work out as Jonah had thought.
2. How did he react?
   Answer: He became angry.
3. What did God ask him?
   Answer: "Do you have a good reason to be angry?"
4. Do you ever have a good reason to be angry with God? Why or why not?

Come together and discuss those three Bible characters and their moods. Talk about how our pouting, depression, and anger affect the people around us. Talk about simple cures for our moods: getting some sleep, eating properly, talking out our frustrations with someone, praying about them, or going for a walk.

Then go to the Lord and see what He has to say. Write Romans 8:28 on the chalkboard. Let a junior higher "teach" the verse to the others. He can do this by asking volunteers to erase a word after each time the group repeats the verse. Soon they will be repeating it with no words to help them.

Discuss how all things that come to them can work together for their good. Stress the word "together," explaining that all things that come to us are not good in themselves, but that our God is so great He can even take things like the unkindness of a friend or an unhappy home situation and make something good come out of them.

Discuss how believing that will result in a thankful attitude, the opposite of a bad mood.

Join hands in a circle and repeat in unison from memory Romans 8:28. Pray that God will help you all to have good moods on the morrow.

What About Friends?

Before the meeting: Enlist four young people to form a panel forum to speak on: (1) how friends can help or harm you, (2) what to do about undesirable friends, (3) how you can be a good friend, and (4) Jesus as best Friend. Work with them so they understand that you will help them by asking questions and that they will also be given the opportunity to question or add ideas.

Say: "Jesus gave us a rule for making friends when He said in Matthew 7:12: 'Therefore whatever you want others to do for you, do so for them.' How would you like to be treated? If you were new at school or church, if you were not established in a group of friends, if you were shy, or if your family had just gone through a death or a divorce." (Discuss.)

How Can We Make Friends?

Discuss Paul's words in Philippians 2:4: "Do not merely look out for your own personal interests, but also for the interests of others."

Divide into twos. Each person is to ask ten questions of his partner, writing down the answers. This is an exercise in friendliness and being interested in the other person. It's also a good way to make friends.

Before doing this, discuss what kinds of questions you might ask a stranger, an acquaintance, and a friend.

Stranger—What's your name? How old are you? How many in your family? What school do you go to?

Acquaintance—What are your favorite subjects in

school? What are your hobbies? What church do you go to?

Friend—What are your future plans? What's your pet peeve? Are you a Christian? What can we do together?

Reassemble, and discuss the advantages and disadvantages of having only one friend.

Advantages—You have someone close to do things with. You really get to know each other.

Disadvantages—You miss out on other good friendships that could be fun and enrich your life. You leave out people who may need your friendship. If your friend leaves or drops you, you're devastated.

Seat your panelists in chairs at the front of the room. Guide the panel to discuss the following:

How Friends Can Help or Harm You

Friends who encourage you to be a better Christian help you.

Friends who draw you away from God harm you.

Friends who come between you and your parents harm you.

Friends who get you into trouble harm you.

Friends who inspire you to do right help you.

What to Do About Undesirable Friends

Invite them to church activities.
Refuse to take part in sinful activities with them.
Pray for them.

How You Can Be a Good Friend

Be a good example.
Encourage him to become a Christian or, if he is already, to grow.
Go out of your way to help him.
Be interested in his affairs, not only your own.
Be honest with him, but also kind.
Pray for him.

My Best Friend, Jesus

Who are His friends? Those who believe in Him and obey Him (John 15:14).

What is it like to have the Son of God for a Friend?

He's always with us—Matthew 28:20.
He loved us enough to die for us—John 14:13.
He understands us—Psalm 147:5.
We can talk to Him about anything—Psalm 142:1-3.
He knows us better than we know ourselves—Psalm 139:13-16.
He has a wonderful plan for us—John 10:10; John 14:3.

You may wish to have the junior highers read these references. Invite any who do not have Jesus as Savior and Friend to stay after the session or talk to you privately at some other time. Use Billy Graham's *Do You Know the Steps to Peace with God?* or Campus Crusade's *Four Spiritual Laws* to lead him to Christ.

What About Peer Pressure?

Before the meeting: Make a copy of the quiz for each youth. Arrange chairs in two long rows, back to back, so kids face opposite walls when they sit in them. Place a quiz and a pencil on each chair.

Peer pressure is one of the greatest difficulties our young people face today. Many of them succumb to it and fall into sinful habits that lead to spiritual, moral, and physical ruin. Start out your discussion on peer pressure with the following quiz. Encourage honesty by assuring your kids that they need not hand in the papers. Instruct them to circle the answer or answers.

Quiz

1. The most important thing to me at school is. . .
    a. to be a good student
    b. to be popular
    c. to have friends

2. The hardest thing for me at school is . . .
    a. to be different
    b. to be unnoticed
    c. to be laughed at
    d. to get my work done
3. The kids at my school . . .
    a. respect Christians
    b. look down on Christians
    c. don't have an opinion
4. I can get along better at school if I . . .
    a. tell kids I'm a Christian
    b. keep quiet about being a Christian
    c. preach to kids about becoming Christians
5. I will go around with . . .
    a. anyone who accepts me, no matter what they do
    b. kids that have the same values as I do
    c. only Christian kids
6. If I am invited to a pot party I should . . .
    a. refuse to go
    b. go and try smoking pot
    c. go and refuse to smoke pot
7. If my friend continues to urge me to do things that
   are wrong I should . . .
    a. keep going around with him/her to try to change
       him/her.
    b. go along with him/her once in a while to keep up
       the friendship
    c. find a different friend
8. How should I act toward kids who are on drugs?
    a. Look down on them.
    b. Try to be friends.
    c. Be friendly, but don't get too close.
9. I can help kids on drugs by . . .
    a. praying for them
    b. inviting them to youth group
    c. going along with them to be a good influence
    d. telling them about Jesus
10. I will be able to withstand peer pressure better if . . .
    a. I talk about the kids who do wrong things
    b. I read my Bible and pray every day
    c. I look down on wrongdoers

After the quiz, ask youth to move their chairs to form a circle. Tell them the story of Daniel and his three friends in Daniel 1—how they dared to be different and were exalted and used by God. Read the story of the three men in the fiery furnace in Daniel 3 as a Scripture dialogue. Choose a narrator to read all that is not dialogue. Shadrach's, Meshach's, and Abednego's speeches, as well as the king's, should be read as dialogue.

Have a sword drill with the following verses to show the folly of being afraid of what people think of us rather than what God thinks: (See chapter 5 for instructions on sword drills.)

Proverbs 29:25
Isaiah 2:11, 22
Daniel 4:35
Daniel 5:23
John 5:44
John 12:42-43

Discuss ways the junior highers can help each other to resist peer pressure: planning fun activities at church, praying for each other, memorizing Bible verses together, and others.

What About the Future?

Many youth today are afraid of the future. They try to drown their fears by taking drugs or alcohol. Suicide among young people is common, because of feelings of hopelessness about today as well as tomorrow. We need to present hope to our young people, hope in Jesus Christ. As a great missionary to Burma said, "The future is as bright as the promises of God."

Pass out slips of paper and pencils to the young people. Ask them to write down one thing about the future that bothers or scares them. Collect the slips, read them to the class, and discuss them briefly. Do not go into the positive aspects of the future at this time.

Pass out slips of paper again and ask young people to write down one good thing about the future. Collect and discuss. This will be your opportunity to talk about God's provision for all our needs, eternal life, and heaven. Use verses from Bible Drill on Future (chapter 7) to lead this discussion.

Now pass out slips and ask each young person to write down at least three things he/she should be doing right now in view of the future. Gather slips and discuss. (Study, learn to work, learn dependability, make friends, save money, learn to know God, learn to pray, be a witness, and so on.)

Divide up into groups of three or four. Give each group five pieces of pipe cleaner six inches long. Ask them to make something together out of the pipe cleaners to illustrate their future. You may want to spark their thinking by suggesting that a triangle could represent God (three-in-one) and a circle could represent eternity (no beginning or ending).

Allow about ten minutes for this activity. Then let each group explain their artwork. You'll be surprised at their creativity.

Conclude with a Bible Drill on the Future (chapter 7). You may have them look up the verses independently or divide them into teams and make it a contest.

Good, Acceptable, Perfect

Wrap a small box in white paper. Print on the top these words: "Study hard, especially English. Practice doing your chores well. Be faithful in your Bible reading every day." Put the small box into a larger box and wrap the larger box in white paper. Print on it: "God's Will: good, acceptable, and perfect" (see Romans 12:2). Wrap another box of approximately the same size and write the same words on it as on the other larger box.

Before class, instruct two of your junior highers to help you present this lesson. Tell one to accept the gift, God's will. The other should protest that he must first see what is in the box before he will accept it. When he is denied the privilege, he refuses the gift.

Leader: God has a gift for you. Jim and Mary, will you come up here? *Hold out boxes to them.* This is a gift from

your King, Jesus. It is His good, acceptable, and perfect
will. It is God's plan for your life.
Both reach out to take the boxes.
Leader: Just a minute. Before you can know God's plan
for you, you must agree to follow it, whatever it may be.
Mary: Let me see what it is—then I'll decide.
Leader: No, you can't do that. God doesn't reveal His will
to those who aren't willing to follow it.
Mary: But God's plan might interfere with my plans.
Leader: Can't you trust Him, Mary? See what it says:
"God's Will: good, acceptable, perfect." Nothing could be
better than that!
Mary shakes her head.
Jim: *Reaches out.* I'll take it.
Leader: If you open up the box you'll find directions for
your first step in God's will.
Jim: *Opens box, takes out the smaller box, and reads
aloud.* Study hard, especially English. Practice doing
your chores well. Be faithful in your Bible reading every
day.
Jim: Is that all? I thought it would be something exciting,
like, "Go to Africa," or, "Join the paratroopers."
Leader: Directions like that will come later when you are
ready for them. They are in the other boxes.
Jim starts to unwrap the next box; the leader stops him.
Leader: No, not yet. God doesn't show us His entire will
all at once. He shows us only one step at a time. After
you have faithfully carried out the first step, He will show
you the next one.
Leader lets Jim and Mary return to their places.

Discuss why young people are afraid to accept God's
will, as Mary was in the skit. (They might have to give up
some cherished plan, some friend; or they might have to
go to a foreign country as a missionary.)

What does our fear of God's will stem from? (Answer:
Doubting God's love and wisdom.)

Look up verses together on God's love and wisdom.

Isaiah 55:8-9
Jeremiah 31:3

Romans 11:33

Look up verses on God's will.

1 Timothy 2:4—Explain that God's will for each of us, first of all, is to be saved. (Explain the way of salvation, if some do not know.)

Proverbs 3:5-6—Explain that God directs those who trust and honor Him.

Jeremiah 29:11—Write this verse on the chalkboard in three parts:

> " 'For I know the plans that I have for
> you,' declares the Lord,
> 'Plans for welfare and not for calamity
> To give you a future and a hope.' "

Divide youth into three groups and have each group take a different portion of the verse each time you repeat the verse until everyone has memorized it.

Remind them that God's will is "good, acceptable and perfect." Discuss what God's will for them in the future might be. Discuss what God's will might be for them right now.

Have silent prayer, giving them a chance to tell God they will accept His will.

Home Is Where the Hassle Is

Divide your junior highers into three groups, according to eye color. Group 1 (brown eyes) will play the part of parents; Group 2 (blue eyes), the part of junior highers; and Group 3 (green or hazel eyes), counselors to bring the two groups together.

Each group will meet together for perhaps ten minutes. Appoint one person in Groups 1 and 2 to be the secretary and to write down the findings on a large sheet of paper.

Group 1 will try to see things from the viewpoint of a parent and write down parents' gripes about their teenagers such as: they don't clean their rooms; they're grumpy when asked to help around the house; they aren't understanding of younger brothers and sisters; they don't appreciate what is done for them, and more.

Group 2 will list gripes they have as teenagers: my

folks treat me like a baby; they don't trust me; they nag; they don't let me watch enough TV; they limit my use of the phone; they don't apologize when they're wrong, and others.

Give Group 3 a slip of paper on which you have written Luke 2:40-52. Ask them to read the biblical account of a family hassle in pre-teen Jesus' life. Discuss the way it was handled. Then discuss possible ways of bringing parents and teens together, such as: have a family session where everyone airs his/her grievances; have household chores written down so kids know what is expected of them; talk about why there is lack of trust; have definite rules for telephone use, and so on.

Groups 1 and 2 will then face each other to bring out their gripes while Group 3 moderates. Of course the leader will be on hand to help Group 3 offer solutions and try to bring understanding between Groups 1 and 2. They will also use the story of Jesus' submission to His parents, recorded in Luke 2:4-42 as a pattern.

Afterwards have the junior highers list on a chalkboard all the good characteristics of their parents they can think of. See who can come up with the most. Emphasize concentrating on the good points instead of the faults. Have all who are willing take part in prayers of thanks for parents. Close by leading in prayer for more understanding between the young people and their parents.

4
On Special Assignment

Youth have an abundance of energy that can be harnessed to accomplish much through special programs and projects. A number of "specials" are suggested here. Some are mere skeletons, and others are fleshed in. You will, no doubt, think of others that suit the particular talents and needs of your junior highers.

Special Program Ideas

Try a puppet show. These two can be used with the youth group or the entire church.

I
You're Invited to My Party

Buy animal puppets if possible—they can be used over and over—or paste pictures of animal faces on paper sacks or stuffed socks. (Freddy must wear a vest.)
Characters: Snazzer the Dog, Rebecca the Rabbit, Minerva the Mouse, Malcolm the Monkey, and Freddy the Monster (All appear except Freddy the Monster.)
Snazzer: Sure, I'll come to your party tonight, Malcolm.
Rebecca: Who else is coming? I mean, you're not inviting Freddy, I hope.

Malcolm: Well, I really didn't want to leave anybody out.
Snazzer: You can leave Freddy out anytime. I wouldn't care one bit. I can't stand him.
Rebecca: He acts so snooty, just like he knows everything.
Malcolm: Well, he's quite an intelligent animal, I'd say.
Snazzer: (shrugs) I hate smart animals.
Malcolm: Why?
Snazzer: I don't know—just because.
Malcolm: Because his smartness makes you feel dumb?
Snazzer: Malcolm, you're insulting me!
Malcolm: No, I'm not. I'm just trying to find out why you don't like Freddy.
Rebecca: The thing I don't like about him is the way he dresses up so snazzy. None of the rest of us has a vest like he does.
Malcolm: What's so bad about a vest?
Rebecca: Well, nothing, really, but he always looks better than I do. It's hard to like somebody that shows you up all the time.
Malcolm: Hm, that's interesting. I'll have to admit the vest has made me a bit envious, too. Has kind of a "now" look, if you know what I mean.
(Animals nod)
Minerva: The thing that gets me down is his bragging. He's always talking about his grandfather winning a blue ribbon in a pet show. Brag, brag, brag. It makes me sick!
Malcolm: Didn't your grandfather ever appear in a pet show?
Minerva: Are you kidding? We mice can't go to things like that. Ladies scream at us. They set out traps for us. Pet show! That's a laugh!
Rebecca: All his talk about pedigree—I don't go for that fancy stuff. We rabbits just multiply and leave it at that. All that pedigree business is stupid, if you ask me!
Malcolm: I think we have a problem here.
Snazzer: You bet we do. Freddy's a problem to all of us.
Malcolm: Oh, I didn't mean *that.* I think *we* have a problem, and it isn't Freddy.
Snazzer: What could *that* be?
Malcolm: It starts with "J."

Minerva: Malcolm, you know I'm no good at spelling.
Rebecca: Maybe the audience would know. What's our problem? Malcolm says it starts with "J"!
Audience: Jealousy!
Snazzer: Jealousy? Is that what you were thinking of, Malcolm?
Malcolm: That's the word.
Snazzer: Well, of all the insults—and I thought you were my friend! You can count me out—I won't be at your party. (He exits.)
Minerva: I'm not coming either, as much as I love parties where I don't have to hide. But I'm not taking any insults from you, Malcolm, even if I am just a little old mouse. (She exits.)
Rebecca: (with her nose in the air) Excuse me, please. You can invite Freddy to your party instead of us. (She exits.)
Malcolm: (sighs) All I did was tell them the truth!
(Pause. Freddy pops up)
Freddy: Hi, Malcolm. You look as glum as I feel.
Malcolm: I am glum. I just got told off by three friends.
Freddy: You're lucky to have three friends. I don't have any.
Malcolm: Why don't you have friends, Freddy?
Freddy: That's what I'd like to know. I try so hard.
Malcolm: How do you try?
Freddy: I got this vest, for one thing, to try to be a little flashy and impress the other animals.
Malcolm: (sighs) You impressed us all right.
Freddy: And I try to act like I know things, so they'll like me. The truth of it is, Malcolm, I don't know much. But don't tell anybody. It's a secret.
Malcolm: You mean you just act like you know a lot?
Freddy: Yes, I'm trying to make friends, you see, and if they know I'm dumb, they might not like me. Please don't tell.
Malcolm: I won't.
Freddy: Another thing I do is brag about my grandfather. He really did win a blue ribbon, but he was the only animal in his category that competed. So it wasn't quite as great as it sounds. And that pedigree business—well, just between you and me, I made it up.

Malcolm: Listen, Freddy, the animals don't care if you're dumb.
Freddy: Huh?
Malcolm: They couldn't care less if your grandfather won a hundred blue ribbons. I mean, it wouldn't make them like you any better.
Freddy: Really?
Malcolm: Your fancy vest isn't what will bring you friends. That just makes them jealous. Maybe I should say it makes "us" jealous.
Freddy: You, jealous of little old me? I can't believe it.
Malcolm: Yes, we do have a little problem there, but you have a problem, too, Freddy. The other animals don't go for your bragging and showing off. If you'd just be yourself—
Freddy: You mean, give up my vest?
Malcolm: Oh, you can keep your vest. But quit acting like you know it all and quit bragging. The animals will like you a lot better if you just act natural.
(Pause while Freddy thinks)
Freddy: Thanks for telling me, Malcolm. You're a true friend, Malcolm. That is, I hope you're my friend. I've never had one before.
Malcolm: Yes, I'm your friend. I'd like to invite you to my party tonight. Can you come?
Freddy: You bet I can! I haven't been invited to a party since—(lowers his voice) the truth is, I've never been invited to a party. I'll go home right now to get ready and touch up my vest. (He exits.)
Malcolm: The two of us might be the only ones at the party, but I don't care.
(Pause. Minerva, Rebecca, and Snazzer reappear.)
Snazzer: Hi, Malcolm.
Malcolm: Well, hi, everybody. You're back!
Snazzer: Yeah, we've been thinking about this jealousy bit. We hate to admit it, but I guess it's true.
Rebecca: We *are* jealous of Freddy, but it's hard to be his friends when he's so snooty.
Minerva: If he'd just stop bragging about his grandfather—
Malcolm: I've got news for you, gang. Freddy isn't going

to be obnoxious anymore. At least he's going to try not to be. You see, he wants friends so badly he's been trying too hard. He really isn't snooty underneath.
Minerva: Isn't he really? And he wants to be my friend?
Malcolm: He sure does.
Rebecca: You invited him to the party, didn't you?
Malcolm: Sure did.
Snazzer: And we're still invited?
Malcolm: You certainly are!
Rebecca: Well, let's try to be really nice to him when he comes.
Malcolm: Sure, let's.
(Freddy appears.)
Animals: Hi, Freddy!
Freddy: Hi, everybody!
(Awkward pause)
Minerva: I—like your vest.
Freddy: Oh, thank you. It's really nothing at all. To be perfectly frank, I picked it up at the dump one day. Somebody had thrown it away. I just cleaned it up. (He laughs nervously.)
Minerva: Hey, maybe I could find a dress or shawl at the dump. A shawl would be better. It wouldn't get in my way when I run away from cats.
Freddy: It's quite possible. Children throw away doll clothes sometimes. I'll even go with you to help you look.
Minerva: Oh, thank you. You're really neat, Freddy. No wonder your grandfather won all those prizes.
Freddy: Well, (coughs) actually my grandfather—
Malcolm: Never mind, Freddy. Let's start our party. Why don't we start with a song? It's very easy, goes like this: (Sing: "Jesus, We Just Want to Thank You," concluding with "Thank You for Giving Us Friends.")

THE END

II
Tongue Trouble

Buy boy and girl puppets or make them out of paper sacks or socks. (Tongue can be a red sock.)

Characters: Jan, Tommy, Tongue
(Jan and Tongue appear.)
Jan: I sure told her a thing or two. Serves her right for being so bossy. Just because she's my big sister—
Tongue: I wish you'd quit making me do things like that.
Jan: Who—who are you?
Tongue: Don't you recognize me? I'm your tongue.
Jan: Oh, yes, I recognize you now. Didn't you like what I said to my sister?
Tongue: I'm really not fond of hurting people. Makes me feel bad—real bad.
Jan: I suppose you didn't like what I said to Mom this morning, either.
Tongue: I certainly didn't! Do you think I enjoy making people cry?
Jan: I don't think I made her cry.
Tongue: That's the trouble with you—you don't think about how people feel. I hate going around like a sword—puncturing balloons, hurting feelings, and piercing hearts. I was made for better things than that.
(Tommy appears.)
Tommy: Pardon me, I just happened to overhear. What's this conversation about, anyway?
Tongue: About me, I suppose—the way I go around cutting people down, hurting their feelings, making them cry. But it's not my fault. Jan's the one in control.
Jan: I didn't realize I was doing all that with my tongue!
Tommy: You're so little. How can you—
Tongue: Don't underestimate me. The Bible says that I'm little, all right, but I have power to start a big fire. That's another name for trouble. It also says I can kill.
Jan: You don't mean it!
Tongue: I don't kill people's bodies, but I can make a shambles of their dreams in a hurry. I can destroy their courage, make them want to give up, and kill their enthusiasm.
Tommy: You wouldn't!
Tongue: I don't want to. Like I said before, I was made for better things.
Tommy: Like what?

Tongue: To encourage people and to make them happy.
Jan: You can do *that?*
Tongue: Sure I can. And wouldn't I love to try it on your mother! She could stand some happiness.
Tommy: What else do you like to do?
Tongue: I like to give kids a boost when they feel sad—like Rick, whose Dad just left.
Jan: You mean you could help Rick?
Tongue: Sure, and Susie, whose mother is in the hospital. I say words, don't I? Words don't only have the power to hurt; they also have the power to heal.
Tommy: Like medicine?
Tongue: Right. I can apply medicine to hurt feelings and broken hearts.
Jan: I had no idea you were so important.
Tongue: I can praise God, too. I really get sick of grumbling all the time.
Tommy: Why do you grumble, then?
Jan: It's my fault. I tell him to. He has to do what I tell him.
Tongue: One of these days I might just go on strike.
Jan: Would you really?
Tongue: It's been done before.
Tommy: You're kidding!
Tongue: No, I'm not. There was this man named Zacharias that we read about in the Bible. God sent an angel to tell him his wife would have a baby.
Jan: Was he glad?
Tongue: Well, he would have been if he'd believed the angel, but he didn't believe him. He said, "That's impossible. My wife and I are too old to have children."
Tommy: Is that why his tongue went on strike?
Tongue: Right. God told his tongue not to say a word until the promised baby was born. The angel said, "Because you haven't believed me, you are to be stricken silent, unable to speak until the child is born."
Jan: I sure hope God doesn't tell you to go on strike! Dear me, I'd have to use sign language if I couldn't talk!
Tongue: Please give me a break, then.
Jan: What do you mean?

Tongue: Let me say kind things instead of nasty ones. Let me heal instead of wounding. Let me encourage people instead of cutting them down. Let me praise God instead of grumbling.
Tommy: What do you say, Jan?
Jan: I—I guess Tongue is right.
Tongue: The first thing I'd like to do is apologize to your mom and sister.
Jan: You mean—say I'm sorry?
Tongue: Yup.
Jan: Do we have to be so extreme?
Tongue: That's where we have to start.
Jan: Oh, dear, this is really hard. What'll I do? (She pauses.) Jesus, will You help me? (She looks up, then pauses again.) OK, I will.
Tongue: Good girl. I feel better already.
Jan: So do I. I haven't felt this happy for ages.
Tommy: I have a feeling everybody around here is going to feel a lot happier now!

THE END

Talent Night

Interest your junior high group in hosting an all-church talent night.

1. Make posters advertising it.
2. Make invitations to be given to each Sunday school class to enlist participants.
3. Arrange as many numbers as possible using junior high kids.
   a. group songs they enjoy, perhaps with guitars
   b. instrumental numbers, group or solo (children who do not play instruments could play the tambourine, triangle, or other simple rhythm instrument.)
   c. speaking choir (assign verses from Psalm 136, *New American Standard Version*, to several good readers, with the speaking choir chiming in on the sentence in every verse, "For His lovingkindness is

everlasting.'' This way you can use everyone, even those not particularly talented.)

4. Choose one or several young people to announce the program.
5. Let the junior highers plan, bring, and serve refreshments for everyone (something simple like brownies, punch, and coffee).
6. Junior highers will act as ushers to take up the offering. Decide beforehand what the offering will go for, so you can announce it: New tables for the fellowship hall? More chairs for the nursery class? Food for the hungry? Your church missionary project? Let them choose, but steer them away from selfish projects, such as a ski trip or a pizza party for themselves.

Theme: God has given all of us abilities to use for Him. A junior higher or a leader can give a short talk on this during the program.

1. The story of the talents—Matthew 25:14-30
    a. Each of us has received at least one ability.
    b. We are responsible to use that ability for God.
    c. If we refuse to use what we have, God will take it from us.
2. The story of the ten minas—Luke 19:12-26
    a. Each one receives the same. (Could this be salvation? Or time?) We are responsible to use and improve it.
    b. What we do with our gifts from God determines our reward.

Your youth will enjoy hosting a talent night, especially if you allow them to do most of the planning themselves with only guidance from you.

Mother-Daughter Tea Ideas

NOSTALGIA THEME
Scriptures about ''remembering'' (Deuteronomy 8:2, 18; Nehemiah 4:14; Psalm 105:5)
Decorations: Antiques, or replicas made from paper (kerosine lamps, a churn, or a bonnet)
Style Show—Old-fashioned clothes

Variation: Have girls model wedding gowns of yester-
years. Speak about love.
Speaker or speakers: "What I Remember About My Christian Mother," "I Remember What God Has Done for Me,"
or "Don't Forget to Remember" (counting our blessings,
thankfulness)

BUTTERFLY THEME
Scriptures about the new birth (John 3:1-16; 2 Corinthi-
ans 5:17)
Decorations: Worms made of egg cartons and butterflies
made of construction paper or crepe paper
Songs about the new birth
Testimonies of being made a new creation in Christ

BREAD THEME
Scripture about Jesus, the Bread of Life (John 6:35)
Decorations: Small loaves of bread sprayed with lacquer
and tied with ribbons (sold after the tea, or saved for
other occasions)
Bread-making demonstration: Give out favorite recipes for
bread or cinnamon rolls.
Talk: "How Jesus Satisfies the Deepest Longings of Our
Hearts"

SEWING THEME
Scripture: Psalm 32:8; Proverbs 31; Jeremiah 29:11
Decorations: Sewing notions
Style Show: Homemade garments and articles (with prizes
for the best ones)
Talk: "God Has a Pattern for Your Life"

BOOK THEME
Scriptures: Psalm 119:97-99, 105, 111, 114; Philippians
4:8
Decorations: Colorful books, reading glasses, and book
jackets
Special Feature: Several reports by girls and mothers of
"A book I liked very much," or "A book that changed my
life"
Talk: "What the Bible Means to Me"

MAY DAY TEA OR SALAD LUNCHEON
Scriptures about spring (Song of Solomon 2:11-12)
Decorations: Pastel-colored tablecloths, gingham-covered
flowerpots, matching May basket nutcups, or May bas-
kets, and support posts decorated like Maypoles (see
chapter 8)
Entertainment: an art exhibit with prizes
Special speaker

Father-Son Activities

1. Overnight Camping Trip with devotions around the
   campfire
2. "Dads and Lads" pancake breakfast with special
   speaker
3. Ping-pong tournament
4. A big-league ballgame
5. Snowcat Showdown with stew cooked over outdoor
   fire
6. A visit to an aquarium or zoo
7. Ice fishing jamboree
8. Track meet, with both sons and fathers participating
9. Bowling party with refreshments afterwards at
   church—"Down Your Alley"
10. Rent a gym for volleyball/basketball
11. "Sports Galaxy"—dinner, sports film, speaker (a
    Christian coach or member of Christian athletic
    organization)

Appreciation Activities

MOTHER'S DAY BRUNCH

Have junior highers make or buy red and white carna-
tions. Present a red one to each mother present whose
own mother is alive, and a white one to each who has lost
her own mother.

Junior highers prepare and serve a simple breakfast for
the mothers before Sunday school or church.

Speak briefly on Proverbs 31:10-31.

DAD'S DAY DINNER

Have a dinner on the grounds after church on Father's Day. Serve fried chicken, potato salad, baked beans, and watermelon or homemade ice cream.

Recognize the youngest father, the oldest father, and the father who has the largest number of children present.

Do the Bible quiz "Which Bible Father . . . ?" (chapter 7).

PRAISE GOD FOR THE PASTOR DAY

Surprise the pastor with an appreciation hour on his anniversary as pastor of the church. Youth and adults whose lives have been touched by him may speak a brief tribute. Invite the congregation to stand in a prayer of support for the pastor.

YOUTH WEEK

You'll like it. During Youth Week, teens step into the role of all adult leadership in the Sunday school and church worship services. They work with the regular adult worker to prepare lessons, sermons, and songs. They learn to usher, play instruments, lead prayers, and give special music. Adult leadership stays close by, in case of an emergency, but they cheer teens on to try their spiritual wings. It's a great growth experience for the future leaders of the church.

RETREAT TO REGROUP

Jesus called His disciples apart to a quiet place for rest and regrouping (Mark 6:31). Youth groups and leaders need this, too.

Webster defines a retreat as "a period of group withdrawal for prayer, meditation, study, and instruction under a leader." Add a bit of fun to this list, and you have a complete plan for a successful youth retreat.

Determine the purpose, the place, and the plan. Then retreat far or near for a long or a short period to refresh and regroup.

A lock-in is a mini-retreat at the church—everybody is locked in the building at a certain hour and spends the night doing most things done at a regular retreat.

Although most lock-in schedules provide for at least a few hours on the bedrolls, rest is usually a neglected item. When the guys and gals are sent to separate rooms for sleeping purposes, they all seem to get bright ideas of what to do with those few hours leaders need for rest. More "creepy-crawlers" come to lock-ins than curling irons!

A sample schedule includes:

1. Supper
2. Orientation—Spell out theme, purpose, and ground rules
3. Songs
4. Worship
5. Snack
6. Discussion
7. Play
8. Sleep (ha, ha)
9. Wake-Up
10. Breakfast
11. Let 'em loose!

FEATURE A FILM

There are many films today that aid in spiritual growth. Feature a film on a regular basis. Follow that with a rap session to reinforce positive teachings.

Consider taking a group to a religious film in town. Hold a viewing party afterwards to discuss the film, and invite youth to make personal commitments to Christ.

Watch a film at a Watch Night Service to see the new year come in. Begin the new year in prayer instead of revelry.

Service Projects

Junior highers will gladly do things for others, if they're

properly guided and motivated. Give them opportunities
to serve.

FOR FREE:

1. Adopt a grandparent.
2. Visit the elderly at nursing homes and sing for them.
3. Babysit without pay for young mothers to free them
   for Bible studies or a much needed break.
4. Do yard work as a team.
5. Clean up the yard of an elderly person—mow grass or
   shovel snow.
6. Garden for God. On an empty lot or garden plot raise
   food to be distributed to the poor in town.
7. Wash windows for a handicapped person.
8. Read to and write letters for a blind person.
9. Volunteer to shop for or with an elderly or handicapped person.
10. Serve tables at a rescue mission fund-raising
    banquet.
11. Lead a campfire service at a resort area.
12. Lead playground activities or a story hour at migrant
    camps, trailer parks, campgrounds, city parks, and
    resort areas. Get permission from authorities first.
13. Help in church Bible school and backyard Bible
    clubs.
14. Tutor a student or refugee who needs help.
15. Work at the church: rake lawn, pick up trash, or
    wash windows.
16. Help a refugee learn English, and American ways.

TO EARN MONEY FOR SPECIAL PROJECTS: HUNGER, CAMP,
CHOIR TRIPS, HOME OR FOREIGN MISSIONS

1. Sponsor a talent night at church with an offering for
   your special project.
2. Plan a "Crazy Dinner" for members of the congregation (see chapter 6). Take up an offering for the
   hungry.
3. Organize a garage sale to raise money for your special
   project or for missions. (Collect salable articles from
   church members.)

4. Put on a bake sale at a local mall.
5. Have a car wash.
6. Conduct a slave auction. Teams of junior highers are "auctioned" for a price, which goes to your project. They then "slave" for their "owners" for a day.
7. Make and sell crafts.
8. Have a cake auction.
9. Collect and sell papers and aluminum cans.
10. Have a "thon" for the Lord. Try a pick-a-thon (pick up litter), a teeter-a-thon, a jump-a-thon, a bike-a-thon, a rock-a-thon, a walk-a-thon, or a job-a-thon.

5
Mission Accomplished

The awards program can have life-changing effects—not only upon junior highers, but also upon those who witness the presentation. A big mission! But it can be accomplished.

World, Here Comes the BYKOTA Brigade!

Kindness is a characteristic foreign to many young people today. In fact, few people of any age are truly kind. Sarcasm, put-downs, "roasts," and "friendly insults" seem to be accepted—even admired—patterns of speech in our society.

This way of life is devastating to a tender self-image. Verbal darts cut deeply into an insecure individual and often cause lasting hurts. This speech pattern is in direct opposition to one of the first Scripture verses we teach our children, "Be ye kind one to another."

Take battle issue with this serious threat to self-worth by organizing an ongoing BYKOTA Brigade. Culminate this campaign for kindness with an awards program, in which you recognize victories over Satan, the commander of the enemy forces. Who knows? Some adults who see the awards program may volunteer to join your brigade!

The BYKOTA Brigade gets its name from the first letter of each word in the kindness theme verse: *"Be Ye Kind One To Another"* (Ephesians 4:32, KJV*). Prepare a felt banner of this verse and use it for the Brigade's motto. If your young people are interested, have them make and wear BYKOTA armbands.

The marching orders for the Brigade are Matthew 28:18-20. Choose a brisk marching song as the Brigade hymn. The following fit the theme well:

"Arise, Oh, Youth of God"
"Serve the Lord in Youth"
"The Banner of the Cross"
"Who Is on the Lord's Side?"
"Loyalty to Christ"
"Dare to Be Brave"
"Stand Up, Stand Up for Jesus"
"We're Marching to Zion"
"Living for Jesus"

Use the BYKOTA Brigade to teach youth to wage defensive and offensive spiritual warfare. Do indepth study of the whole of Ephesians 4:32, focusing not just on the BYKOTA phrase, but equally upon the "tenderhearted" and "forgiving" elements.

Search the Scriptures for related verses. Consider these references.

OFFENSIVE WEAPONS	DEFENSIVE WEAPONS
Psalm 19:14	Psalm 34:13
Psalm 35:14	Proverbs 12:18
Psalm 140:3	Proverbs 15:1
Proverbs 15:23	Matthew 12:36
Proverbs 31:26	Romans 13:12
Mark 4:14	Galatians 5:19-24
Luke 6:35	Ephesians 4:29
John 6:68	Ephesians 6:11, 13
Galatians 5:14	Ephesians 5:6
2 Timothy 2:15	2 Thessalonians 2:17

* King James Version.

Hebrews 3:13 2   Timothy 2:4
James 1:22
James 3:8

Teach your young people to use the "Sword of the Spirit" by having sword drills. Conduct the drill as follows. Line them up side by side, each with his Bible. At the "Attention" command they stand with arms and Bible at their sides. "Draw swords" means they raise arms waist-high with the closed Bible on one open palm and the other open palm resting flat on top of the Bible. Right-handers place their right hand on top of the Bible; left-handers place their left hand on top.

State the Bible reference slowly. Repeat the reference. Declare, "Charge!" Young people open Bibles, find the verse, place an index finger on it, and step forward. Call upon the first one forward to state the reference and read the verse. All then step back in the straight line, and you begin again: "Attention, draw swords [reference], charge!"

With practice, your Brigade will get so fast they will amaze you. They learn just how far down on their thumbs the various books of the Bible open to.

You may want to begin drilling by concentrating on knowing the order of the books of the Bible (see chapter 3 for songs to help them learn the order the books come in—also chapter 8 for "Bible Town"). Conduct Bible book drills by calling a book title instead of chapter and verse. (When they "charge" they must find the book named—with index finger on chapter 1, verse 1—step forward, and name the book before and the book after, without looking them up. They do not read a verse in this drill, but simply test their memory and skill at finding the books.)

Focus on memorizing the Word. Brigaders won't always have a Bible on hand when attacked by the enemy. Try the following methods to aid in committing verses to head and heart use.

1. Make flash cards with verses on one side and references on the other.
2. Print verses on an overhead projector. Flash a com-

plete verse. Then cover all but the reference. Recall
the verse aloud in unison. If the group falters,
uncover part of the verse and try saying it in unison
again.
3. Enlist a musically talented youth to set a verse to
music. Teach the simple tune to the group. Sing it
often. Many Bible verses have already been set to
music by professionals. Sing those.
4. Chart a verse artistically on colored paper with vari-
colored letters. Cut around the shape of the letters as
illustrated. Put a verse or two on a focal wall each
week. Repeat it in unison. Change the verses weekly,
but recall aloud verses from the previous weeks.
5. Have a verse spell-down. Form two teams and follow
the spelling bee format, calling out a reference to one
team and then the other.
6. Have a sword drill by memory. Line up junior highers
without their Bibles. Call out the reference twice and
say, "Charge!" Have the first one to step out say the
verse. Give individual points for correctly spoken
verses.
7. Reward those who learn verses with praise and some
simple inexpensive prize that aids in Bible learning.
8. Spend a few minutes saying a verse each time you
gather.
9. Have a sword duel. Select two who have memorized
well to challenge each other to a verbal duel. The
Scripture says the Word of God is sharper than a
two-edged sword. See which young people can thrust
swords (verses) the longest.
10. Use a dart board to encourage memorizing. Team up
a good dart thrower with a good memorizer. Call out
a verse reference. If the memorizer knows it, he and
his dart-throwing partner ask to try for a bull's-eye.
Give points both for the verbal dart and the physical
dart.
11. Promote memorizing with puppet skits and announce-
ments. Puppets could even have a verse spell-down,
in Punch and Judy fashion.
12. Relate facts that can be memorized with association

clues. For instance, learn the names of the twelve disciples this way. Begin with the first two letters of the alphabet.

A stands for Andrew.
B is for Bartholomew.
There are five J's:
    John,
    James,
    James,
    Judas,
    and Judas Iscariot.
Skip two letters of the alphabet, K and L.
M stands for Matthew.
Skip two letters, N and O.
There are two P's, Peter and Philip.
Skip two letters, Q and R.
S is for Simon.
There are two T's, Thomas and Thaddaeus.

Go creative in your battle for kindness. Sponsor a BYKOTA banner or poster contest. Unkind words are sometimes referred to as velvet darts, verbal razors, and soft barbs. Those terms might suggest a colláge. Verses that might lend themselves to unusual posters or banners include: Psalm 28:7; Psalm 57:5; Proverbs 5:4; and Jeremiah 9:8. Your young people may think of other verses to illustrate. Any art mediums could be used in making the banners or posters.

Post youth-made slogans around the church (with permission, of course). Possibilities are: "Kindness counts," "Put down the put-downs," "Friendly insults aren't friendly," "Cut out the cutdowns," "Ban the burn," "Tame the tongue," "Rout the roast," and "Sarcasm is sick." Add BYKOTA in small print to each. Adults will ask what your code word means, and youth can state a positive truth.

Being AWOL (absent without leave) is a "no-no" for Brigaders, so recognize youth for perfect attendance. Do "arms check" each meeting time to keep record of those who bring their Bibles, the Sword of the Spirit. Grant rank to those who memorize verses and do kind deeds.

Promote kind deeds as well as kind words. Recall the story of Peter and John's healing the lame man (Acts 3:1-11). Remind youth that Jesus said to give alms (good deeds, in their case) in secret and God would reward them openly (Matthew 6:1-4).

Ask youth to give you their "reporting for duty" good deed results in secret—on paper or in your ear. Give them individual positive reinforcement for any kindness shown. Do not embarrass them by naming names or deeds publicly.

Keep a record of Brigader achievements. At the awards program recognize "captains," perfect attenders, and any other accomplishments you have chosen to promote.

Do have a sword drill demonstration for parents on Awards Night. Display the banners and posters, appropriately ribboned according to winner, in the fellowship hall during refreshment time.

A suggested outline for Awards Night Program:

Invocation
Hymn
Explanation of BYKOTA
Sword Drill
Recognition of Brigaders
Charge to Church (to follow BYKOTA Brigade's example)
Commitment Prayer
Refreshments

6

Diversionary Tactics

All work and no play makes for a dull day, so we offer these diversions. Food is very important to junior highers. These party plans center on stuffing the natives to keep them happy.

Some ideas are self-explanatory. Others need a bit of illuminating.

1. Forecasting Chili Today, Hot Tamale—Serve south of the Border favorites.
2. Steak Fry—tube steaks, that is. Translation: weiners.
3. Have a "Corny Ball"—Make and enjoy popcorn balls.
4. Burger Bash—Build your own burgers.
5. Bucket Brigade and Suds—a Spring Cleaning Party with root beer floats.
6. Fondue some Fun.
7. Appealing Sweetly for your Presence—Savor some caramel apples.
8. Lean into a Pizza Party—Thaw frozen bread dough, shape unique pizza crusts, and top with your junior highers' favorite assortments.
9. Round Steak á la Economy. Translation: bologna sandwiches.

10. Taffy Pull

11. Super Sundae—Bring the makings for ice cream sundaes. Each creates his own gastronomical delight (see origin of this sweet treat below).

12. Split a Banana—Build a giant banana split in a wooden trough lined with foil.

13. Super Salad Supper—Toss a salad from a smorgasbord of vegies and trimmings brought by youth.

14. International Taste Teasers—Serve dishes from around the world.

15. Watermelon Feed

16. Fish Fry

17. Stir up a Stew—Plan an Irish-stew hobo party with each person bringing either a carrot, an onion, or a potato and a clean tin can to eat out of. Leader gets stew meat boiling in a big pot, preferably over a campfire. Hobos add their cut-up food contribution to the pot and play games while the stew cooks. Assign food items so you have more potatoes, fewer carrots, and just a few onions.

18. Tacorific Piñata Party—Make a piñata for a different Christmas party (see chapter 8). Menu? Tacos, of course.

19. Potato Party—Have each person bring a raw, clean, foil- wrapped potato as his "ticket" to the party. Do fun and games while potatoes bake. Smother hot potatoes with assorted toppings: cheese, bacon bits, butter, sour cream, chives, chopped eggs, etc. Enjoy!

20. Pretzel Party—Mix pretzel batter, and shape pretzels into any form desired. Study or play something while they rise. Then bake and eat.

21. Bar-B-Q and Brownies Cookout.

22. Have a BLAST. Translation: *Buffet with Laughs And Straight Talk.*

23. Fifth Quarter Huddle—Food and fellowship after the football game.

24. Progressive Dinner—A several-course dinner with each course served in a different home, preferably far enough apart for food to settle some before the next stop.

25. Sumptuous Spaghetti Supper
26. Pizzaburger Party
27. Shakes-a-Plenty—Make your own milkshakes.
28. Love that Lasagna.
29. Messy Josés (Pronounced: *hoe-says*). Translation: Sloppy Joes.
30. Fireplace Fun—Pop some corn, then roast weiners and marshmallows in the fireplace.
31. Dough-Re-Mi—Sing-a-long plus a biscuit-making contest.
32. Corn You Lettuce Carrot Where You've Bean?—A "Seedy Social" to accompany your Garden for God project. Serve hot buttered corn and raw vegies with dips.
33. Marshmallow Madness—Feed 'em Relay; Art 'em; Eat 'em—plain, in hot chocolate, or in "S'mores" (roasted marshmallow and a piece of chocolate between two graham crackers). Yummy!
34. Crank up some Cream—Homemade ice cream, that is.
35. Progressive Meal Hike—Follow walking orders and eat what you find left ahead of time at prescribed stops.
36. Croquet 'N Cookout
37. Canoe and Catch—Broil fish caught while canoeing.
38. Clambake
39. Ski 'N See (what's in the basket you brought).
40. Galloping Gourmet—Picnic after horseback riding.
41. Box Supper—Auction off unlabeled boxes and eat what's inside, with the young lady who prepared it.
42. Coast 'N Roast—Roast weiners in a sheltered spot or indoors after sledding, tobogganing, Snow-Catting, or innertubing.
43. Tenth Inning Stretch—Serve peanuts, popcorn, and pink lemonade after the softball or baseball game.
44. Loll around at a Luau. Go Hawaiian and enjoy fresh pineapple and coconuts, mangoes, and papayas. Be really authentic and roast a pig!
45. Try some menu madness. Have a "crazy dinner."

Crazy Dinner

Your junior highers will love hosting a "crazy dinner"

for the adults. If your church is large you may want to
limit it to a certain group in the church: young adults,
senior citizens, Sunday school teachers, or parents. If
your church is small, all the adults can be invited.

Plan a menu together, or use the one suggested. If you
plan your own you will have to make up "crazy" names
to call the different items you are serving.

Mimeograph menus with the "crazy" names. The guests
are to number the menu items in the order they want to
receive them. Because they're not sure what the menu
items mean they may get their spaghetti before they get
their forks and have to eat it with their knives or fingers.
Some may unwittingly order their dessert before their
main course. Whatever happens, it's hilarious. Your
young people will enjoy filling the orders and watching
the expressions on the faces of the guests when they serve
them.

Pass the hat at the end of the meal for donations to pay
for the food and for the special project the youth are working towards.

Sample Menu: Crazy Dinner

Choose four items for each course. List each item only
once. It's not fair to borrow anything from your neighbor.
Those leaving food on their plates must help with the
dishes. Utensils may be kept for the rest of the meal *once*
they have been received. Youth will assume the responsibility for transportation to the nearest hospital if necessary. Enjoy yourself!

Menu

1. Excavator
2. I Yell
3. Pitch
4. Long Johns
5. Dumb Joke
6. Hair Knot
7. Peter Rabbit Special
8. A Jam
9. Complexion

10. Measure of Gold
11. Exact Fit
12. Lover's Joy
13. Wages
14. Juicy Beans
15. Fish Delight
16. Sharp Cookie

Codes: Excavator—toothpick; I Yell—ice cream; Pitch—fork; Long Johns—spaghetti; Dumb Joke—corn; Hair Knot—bun; Peter Rabbit Special—coleslaw; A Jam—pickle; Complexion—olive; Measure of Gold—carrot; Exact Fit—tea; Lover's Joy—spoon; Wages—celery; Juicy Beans—coffee; Fish Delight—water; Sharp Cookie—knife.

Origin of the Sundae

At the turn of the century in Evanston, Illinois, a group of very pious churchmen forbade the sale of ice cream sodas on Sunday. They thought that the carbonated soda was a corrupting influence on the people.

To get around the law, some ice cream parlors began serving ice cream with syrup, but without soda. They called these sodaless ice cream treats "Sunday sodas." People liked the new dish and soon began asking for "Sundays" all through the week.

Some church person objected to the dish's being named after the Lord's Day, so its spelling was changed to "sundae." Now this once forbidden treat is popular around the world.

7

Maneuvers on Location

A maneuver, according to Webster, "is a procedure or method of working usually involving expert physical movement . . .an action taken to gain a tactical end."

Games played in or around the location of your youth department offer a means to several ends. Why play games with your junior highers?

1. Physically, young teenagers need to move around. Sitting still actually *hurts,* during this quick growth spurt.
2. Constructive use of their energy prevents disruptive behavior.
3. Games are a great teaching tool.
4. Teachers and young people who play together stay together. You don't want to try to keep up with them or show them up, but having fun with them helps you to really know them. It shows them that you are a real person, and it offers you an opportunity to show them that Christians can do many things for fun without compromising their standards.

Crowd Breakers

Have you several visitors at your youth meeting? Try

one of these mixers to break up the crowd and to make
new friends.

Pass out pencils and slips of paper listing the following
items. The kids will mingle and fill them out.

1. Wears size 12 shoes
2. Lives in a town that begins with F
3. Has Indian ancestry
4. Has spoken German
5. Grew up on a farm
6. Has lived in more than four states
7. Has lived in a foreign country
8. Has blue eyes
9. Was born in December
10. Has been a Christian five years
11. Likes chocolate cake
12. Can play a musical instrument
13. Can ski
14. Is in the eighth grade
15. Is not wearing blue jeans

YOU'RE HUMMING MY SONG

Get acquainted and form groups at the same time. Give
out strips of paper listing well-known song titles. Distribute four different titles if you want to form four
groups. Instruct each person not to show his song title to
anyone. Instead, he is to wander around the room humming the tune of his song until he finds all the others who
are humming his song.

Then the hummers will congregate (by song) into cor-
ners, neatly and pleasantly grouped for the next activity.

BYKOTA INITIALS

Form a circle sitting in chairs or on the floor. Meet the
person on your right. Going around the circle, have each
youth introduce himself and the person on his right. To
introduce correctly he will say the first and last name and

a kind remark that begins with the initials of the first and last name of his new friend.

Example: "This is Paul Spencer. He's pretty special."

Continue around the circle until each person has introduced his neighbor.

Indoor Games

TOMFOOLERY

Players sit in a circle on the floor. Choose one person to be "it." He begins by doing something to the person on his right (nudges, or makes a face, perhaps). That person must do the same thing to the person on his right, and so on around the circle until it comes back to the leader, who then must do something different, which again must be copied around the circle.

This goes on until someone laughs. The one who laughs then becomes "it" and must start the tomfoolery.

BALLOON FUN

Choose sides and number. Sides face each other about six feet apart. Even numbers exchange places, so that every other player belongs to the other team. Have two balloons of different colors, like green and yellow.

At the signal to start, the one at the head of the green side bats his balloon to his team member across from him, who bats it back to the next team member across from him. The yellow does the same to his teammate. The balloons are batted in order to the end of the line and then back again.

The team that gets its balloon back to the starting place first wins. If the balloon touches the floor, it must be started over again at the beginning of the line. It is against the rules for anyone to touch the opposing team's balloon.

BALLOON RELAY

Have an equal number of players on each side. Line up as for a relay, facing the goal line. Give the person at the head of the line a spoon and a balloon. At the "go" signal, he must maneuver his balloon to the goal line, without touching it with anything but his spoon. After he has reached the goal line, he carries the balloon and spoon back to his next teammate, who takes his turn, and so on.

The side that finishes first wins.

BALLOON VOLLEYBALL

This is safe to play inside your youth room. Play like regular volleyball, but use a smaller "court" and a balloon for a ball. Blow up several balloons, in case of bursts.

HANDY RACE

Choose two sides. Team members hold hands, and teams face each other. The lead man passes a tennis ball to the one next to him, who must receive it without unclasping his hands and pass it to the next person the same way. If the ball drops, it must be retrieved by the one who dropped it—without anyone's unclasping hands—and continue on from where it was dropped.

The team that gets the ball to the end first, wins. Or you may want to have it go up and down the line several times.

SHOEBOX RELAY

Have two shoeboxes (without covers) for each team. The players of a team are divided: half stand at the starting line and half at the finish. At the signal, the first player of each team places one of his shoeboxes on the floor and steps in it with his left foot, holding his right foot up in the air. Then, without letting his foot touch the floor, he places the second shoebox down and steps into that with his right foot.

In this way, he advances across the room to where his teammates wait to take a turn in returning to the starting point in the same manner. If a player loses his balance and touches the floor with his hand, or his foot that is not in the box, he must start over. The team that finishes first wins.

WHO'S THE ROBBER?

Pass out slips of paper to each player. All will be blank except one, which has the word *Robber* written on it. Players stand in a circle behind their chairs. The object of the game is to discover who the "robber" is before he "robs" everyone. When the "robber" winks at a player, the player must cry out, "I've been robbed!" and slump into his chair, without giving any indication of who the "robber" is. He is then out of the game until the next round.

The players must watch each other carefully to try to find out who is winking. If one of them sees the "robber" wink at another player, he shouts out who the robber is. The game then starts all over again with fresh slips of paper and a new "robber." Some players are very clever at winking unobtrusively; others are very obvious. It's lots of fun.

ABC GAME

Print letters of the alphabet on small cards. Have the group sit in a circle. Choose one person to be "it." He flashes a card before the group. The first one to say a word beginning with that letter gets the card. The person who has the most cards at the end of the game wins. (To make it more difficult, require the kids to give adjectives beginning with the letter and then, later, try verbs.)

TO TOWN WE GO!

Put two sets of old clothes in two suitcases: pants, shirt, jacket, hat, boots, and gloves. Instruct junior highers to form two lines for a relay, across from the suitcases. Each player must run to the suitcase, open it, put on all the clothes, take them off, put them into the suitcase, and shut the suitcase. He then goes back to his team and touches the hand of the next player.

The first team to finish wins.

SOMETIMES UP, SOMETIMES DOWN

Put two folding chairs on the floor, some distance from

your two lines of kids. Players must run to the chair, open it, sit on it, fold it up, lay it back on the floor, run back to his team, and touch the hand of the next contestant.

The line that finishes first wins.

LET'S GO TO THE ZOO

Seat kids in a circle on chairs. Assign five animals to the youth this way: all those whose first name starts with letters from A to D are alligators; those from E to H are elephants; I to M, are monkeys; from N to R, rhinoceroses; S to V, tigers; and W to Z, zebras. Write the groups on the chalkboard or a large card to refresh their memory.

"It" has no chair, but he tries to get one. He calls out the names of two or more animals, and all in those categories must scramble for different seats. The one left without a seat becomes "it." If "it" wants everyone to change places, he calls, "Let's go to the zoo!" and everyone must scramble for a different seat.

PAT'S PINEAPPLE PUNCH

This is a variation of "Fruit Basket Turnover." Seat the teens in a circle, with no empty chair for you, the leader. The leader will name each person an ingredient that could be put in a punch. He may name several persons the same ingredient.

Tell the group you will mix your punch with their help. As you add their ingredients they are to follow you as you move around stirring it up inside the circle, telling your made-up story of putting the punch together. Instruct them to listen for their names. When you say, "Pat's Pineapple Punch," everyone must change chairs while the leader scrambles to find an empty chair. The chairless one is the next leader, who may or may not rename the ingredients. The leader may call out, "Pat's Pineapple Punch" at any time.

Vary the game according to seasons or party theme by changing the made-up story. It can be punch for any time of the year. For Halloween it should include such delicacies as "bat's toenails," "blood," and "poison."

The game can also name things packed for camp, sights

seen on a vacation, models of cars passed on the highway, or even foreign words or phrases for a missionary party. Since the story is "made-up," this active game is super-adjustable. The phrase that causes all the players to move will change according to the story plan chosen.

Instead of the traditional bobbing for apples, try this one. Put paper towels on the floor and an apple, pear, or peach on each one. Players must eat the fruit without touching it with their hands. Pears and peaches work best, because of their softness.

Variation: Hang several of these fruits on strings in the doorway of your party room. The youth cannot enter until they have taken a bite from the swinging fruit. Smart ones will team up on opposite sides of the fruit to hold it still enough to bite into!

"Uncle George" can be a girl or a boy who lies on a bed or cot with his feet at the head of the bed. Put covers up around his feet, a mask on his feet, and a hat to make his feet look like his head. Cover Uncle George's head at the foot of the bed and put shoes on his hands, which will stick out of the covers.

Bring kids in one at a time to visit Uncle George. Have them sit by his "head" (really his feet). Tell them they must be very quiet because Uncle George is extremely ill.

All at once Uncle George sits up and screams. That usually evokes a scream from the visitor, too, who is not expecting Uncle George's head to suddenly appear from the foot of the bed.

This is a good Halloween game, when everyone expects to be frightened a little.

Instruct the youth that you are going to have a stargazing session. To give it a scientific flavor, inform them that there are 100 billion stars in our galaxy and 200 billion or more in other galaxies. Take each person into a separate room to "see the stars" through the sleeve of an old coat.

As each kid peers up into the sleeve, pour a small amount of water down the sleeve onto his face. Make each one promise that he will not disclose "the secret of the stars" to the other players who follow.

RHYTHM

Sit in a circle on chairs. Number chairs for as many as are playing. Number 1 leads the group in rhythm. Slap knees, clap hands, snap fingers on right hand, clap hands. Now you are ready to repeat it. On the snap of the finger, number 1 calls his own number, and on the next snap another number—12, for instance. Keeping in rhythm, Number 12 says his number at the next snap of the fingers and someone else's number on the next rhythmic snap. Each must respond on the very next snap, keeping the "slap, clap, snap, clap" rhythm going.

When one fails to say a number on the snap when his number is called, he must go to the end of the line. Each person moves up to fill in where the person has vacated and changes his number according to the number of the chair. The object is to get to the head of the line, to seat number 1, and stay away from the tail.

Great fun! They probably won't want to stop!

ANIMAL RHYTHM

Sit in a circle so all can see each other. Leave elbow room. Designate one animal to each chair position and review the animal signs. The number 1 animal always begins the game. He signs his animal and then another animal sign. The animal "called" must react in rhythm, signing his own animal and then someone else's. Anyone who misses goes to the last chair, and the others move up, assuming the animals of the chairs they moved to. The object of the game is to become the number 1 animal.

To make the animal signs, try to enact the animals' appearances, as described below. Twenty-one animals are given. If fewer than twenty-one play, choose the animals you like best. Number 1 is always the elephant.

1. Elephant—Cross arms; one hand goes up to pinch nose, while the other arm hangs straight like a trunk.
2. Aardvark—Extend right arm straight, fingers down. Wriggle fingers while touching nose to extended right arm.
3. Chicken—Hang thumbs under armpits; flap wings.
4. Monkey—Scratch ribs with both hands.
5. Frog—Bounce heel of right hand off right knee, like a frog leaping into a pond.
6. Giraffe—Hold one arm straight up like a long neck.
7. Unicorn—One forefinger makes a horn above center forehead.
8. Peacock—One arm fans in a circle, like a peacock's tail.
9. Moose—Place both thumbs against side of head with fingers raised like antlers.
10. Fish—Place palms together and "swim" away from body.
11. Snake—Right arm wriggles outward.
12. Bull—Two forefingers form horns on top of head.
13. Owl—Form two circles around eyes with forefinger and thumb. Stretch middle fingers to touch cheeks.
14. Shark—Place right hand on left shoulder and left hand under opposite armpit. Open and close the "mouth" formed.
15. Kangaroo—Bend arms up against body like small front paws. Wriggle fingers of the "paws."
16. Alligator—Raise one arm over head, with the other arm low. Close with a snap by slapping palms together in front of the body while keeping arms straight.
17. Horse—Slap hands 1-2-3 against thighs.
18. Goat—Pull against the chin like a goatee.
19. Donkey—Cup hands on head like big ears.
20. Eagle—Extend arms wide from side. Flap like wings.
21. Duck—Flap hands to make a bill in front of your mouth.

A fun game that calls for quick, alert teens. Even more fun than the original rhythm—and quieter, too.

WHERE IN THE WORLD?

Sit in a circle. The first teen says the name of a place (city, country, continent, lake, ocean, mountain). The next one must say the name of a place that begins with the letter the first place ended with. For instance, Number 1 says, "Brazil." Number 2 can say, "Lapland"; number 3, "Detroit"; and so on.

PICTURE PRETTY

One youth must be in on the secret of this game. He goes out of the room, and the leader announces that he will take a picture of one of them in a spoon. The group, sitting in a circle, chooses which teen he should take a picture of. He stands in front of that person and pretends to take a picture, then calls in his partner.

While his partner looks at the spoon intently, the leader sits down, trying to sit as much as possible like the one whose picture he has taken. The partner guesses who it is by looking at the leader and then around at the others. Everyone is amazed when he guesses correctly.

After doing it several times, someone might have caught on. Let him try. If nobody catches on, quit the game and save the mystery for another time.

DRAW A CHRISTMAS CAROL

Divide into two sides. Each side chooses a Christmas carol. Side Number 1 sends a representative to Side Number 2 to find out what their choice is. Then, he has two minutes to "draw" the carol on a large piece of paper or the chalkboard. While he draws, his side tries to figure out from his picture (no words) what song he is trying to portray. If they guess right within two minutes, they gain a point.

Repeat the procedure with the Side Number 1's song being portrayed by a representative from Side Number 2. Change representatives each time for maximum participation.

You'll be surprised at how many artists you have!

THE WIND BLOWS

Pick an accomplice who knows the secret of the game. Have young people sit in a circle. Tell them you and your partner have known each other so long you have begun to think alike. Ask them if they'd like you to demonstrate your think-alike ability. Tell them you will send your partner from the room and see if he/she can identify the person you pick out while he is out of the room.

The partner leaves, and you darken the room, leaving only enough light for you to distinguish people's identities.

Place your hands over any head you choose and call out to your partner in the next room, "The wind blows." Partner calls back, "Blow on." You move to another person, moving in any direction, repeating, "The wind blows." Partner responds, "Blow on." Continue this process until you place your hands over the head of the chosen one. Say, "The wind blows and rests upon." If you have your signals straight, your partner should be able to correctly name the person you have your hands over, even though he is still outside the room.

The group will puzzle much over your thinking process and will doubtless need many demonstrations. Alter your selection order, sometimes going directly to the chosen person, skipping over persons, or even going almost completely around the circle.

When an individual thinks he knows the secret, invite him to be the partner. Do not tell the secret, and this game will remain a fascination until every person has figured it out.

The secret? The person the wind rests upon is the person who speaks last before your partner leaves the room!

Outdoor Games

TREASURE HUNT

This is a good team activity when the weather is fine. Enlist the help of several of your junior highers to set it up if you have a large group. Otherwise, do it yourself and let all participate in the hunt. You will need to make up clues to guide the searchers to the treasure. Use rhymes if possible. For instance:

I point the way to folks who pass Invite to church and Sunday school class.

The clue is taped to the church sign. When they find this clue, another rhyme will lead them to the next. Perhaps it will be:

When Pastor needs to visit the sick, I'm necessary—you know? Be quick.

The clue will be somewhere on the pastor's car.

You can have two separate treasures and two sets of clues, or just one treasure and two sets of clues to find it. Be careful not to put clues for different teams too close to one another, as this creates confusion. The treasure can be balloons or some edible treat.

KEEP AWAY

This simple ball game is always a favorite and a good way to use up excess energy. Girls against the boys works best. Each side tries to keep the ball away from the other. They must keep throwing it to their teammates and not hold it. A rubber or sponge ball is best for this.

SCAVENGER HUNT

Divide up your group into teams of three or four people. Give each team a list of articles to find. The list will vary according to the time of year and your locale, but here are some suggestions:

a pine cone
a maple leaf
piece of moss
a picture of Abraham Lincoln (on a penny)
a hair from a redhead
something alive (insect or animal)

a flower
a berry
a picture of an eagle (on a quarter)

The team that finds all the articles first wins.

WATER, WATER EVERYWHERE!

Line up in teams for this exciting relay. Put a bucket of water at the head of each line and a quart jar at the tail. Give the first youth of each team a paper cup. At the "go" signal, he will dip water out of the bucket with his cup and pass it down the line to the last player, who will pour it into the jar and then run to the front of the line with the cup and become the one who dips and passes the second cup of water. The team that fills their jar first wins.

Better play this one on a warm day, as there will be plenty of spills!

JUNIOR HIGH OLYMPICS

Have an old-fashioned track meet with assorted races, jumps, and throws.

WHEELBARROW RACE

Each contestant chooses a partner. One is the wheelbarrow, walking on his hands while his partner holds his feet and "wheels" him to the finish line and back.

THREE-LEGGED RACE

The right leg of one racer is tied to the left leg of his partner, around the ankle. They run with their "three legs" to the finish line and back.

Variation: Try a four-legged race. There are three members to each team. The one in the middle has his right leg tied to the left leg of the one on his right, and his left leg tied to the right leg of the one on his left. The first trio to reach the finish line, with legs still tied together, wins. The secret is to go slowly and carefully, one step at a time. In this race, the slowest usually wins.

SOMERSAULT RACE

Somersault to the finish line forward, then backward.

BROAD JUMP RELAY

Two teams line up behind a starting point. The first player on each side jumps as far as he can at the "go" signal. The next player rushes to where the first player has landed and jumps from there as far as he can. The third player then jumps from where the second player has landed and so on until everyone has jumped. The team that has covered the most distance wins.

Variations: Jump backwards, one foot forward (a hop), or flat-footed.

JUMP A ROPE

Two leaders hold a rope while youth form a line and take turns jumping over it. The rope will be slightly raised each time, until it is quite high. Those who touch it while jumping must drop out.

EGG TOSS

Play this one in old clothes. Each player picks a partner. Give each pair one raw egg. Partners stand about eight feet apart. At a given signal, the player with the egg throws it to his partner, who catches and returns it. After each turn, players take one step backwards—away from their partners. The team that keeps the egg from breaking for the longest time wins. It's surprising how long an egg can stay intact, if thrown and caught correctly.

Variations: Discus throw—use a paper plate; Feather throw; Shot-put—use a big, round balloon.

Bible Games

BIBLICAL CHARADES

Act out events of the Old and New Testaments. Give junior highers a description of the event to be enacted, or just the Bible reference. (It would be a better learning

experience if they are given only the reference to look up.)
They may work individually or in groups.

A few interesting events to charade are: Eve is created
(Genesis 2:21-22); David kills Goliath (1 Samuel 17:45-
51); Samson gets a haircut (Judges 16:17-21); the bor-
rowed axehead swims (2 Kings 6:5); friends lower the paralyzed man through the roof to Jesus' feet (Mark 2:3-5);
the Good Samaritan helps the wounded man (Luke 10:30-
35); and Paul gets bitten by a snake (Acts 28:3).

BIBLE TWENTY QUESTIONS

Divide into two teams. Each team selects a person or
thing from the Bible. For instance, Team 1 may choose
"Noah's Ark." The other team tries to find out what they
have chosen by asking questions that can be answered by
"yes" or "no." To begin, they should discover if it is
"animal, vegetable, or mineral." Noah's Ark would be in
the vegetable category, because it was made from trees.
Another key factor would be "Old or New Testament."

Team 2 tries to find the answer by asking twenty questions or less. If they exceed twenty questions, they must
give up until their next turn. Then Team 2 chooses something from the Bible, and Team 1 asks the questions.

Note: It may be well to have one adult on each team, if
possible.

BOOK REVIEWS

Divide group into two sides. Each youth must take his
turn to answer the question you ask about the Bible. If he
answers correctly, give him a button (1 point); if incor-
rectly, a slip of paper (-1 point). If the one whose turn it is
cannot answer, another person on his side may volunteer.
If he does not know the answer, give the other team a
chance. At the end of the game add up the buttons and
subtract the slips of paper to see which side wins.

Questions are quickies like these:

History—They must give the name of a book in this category, such as "Esther."
Job—They must give the category: "Poetry."

A book in the Old Testament with two parts—1 and 2
Samuel, Kings, or Chronicles.
A book in the New Testament with three parts—1, 2, and
3 John.
Prophecy in the New Testament—Revelation.
Ezekiel—They must give the category: "Major prophet."

BIBLE BASEBALL

Divide into two teams. Set up three bases and home
plate in a large room or outdoors. Ask quiz questions of
the team "up to bat." If the player answers correctly he
takes a base. If not, he's out. After three "outs," the other
team is "up to bat." Count only those who reach "home."
You may want to make up your own questions. Here are
some samples:

1. Who was the first baby born into the world?
   Answer: Cain.
2. Who built the Ark?
   Answer: Noah.
3. Who was the father of the Jewish nation?
   Answer: Abraham.
4. Who was cheated into marrying the sister of the girl
   he loved?
   Answer: Jacob.
5. Who gave his favorite son a coat of many colors?
   Answer: Jacob.
6. Who was sold by his brothers?
   Answer: Joseph.
7. What baby was put in a basket in the river?
   Answer: Moses.
8. Who found him?
   Answer: Pharaoh's daughter.
9. Who was Moses' sister?
   Answer: Miriam.
10. Who killed Goliath?
    Answer: David.
11. Who was Israel's first king?
    Answer: Saul.

12. Who asked God for wisdom to rule Israel?
    Answer: Solomon.
13. Who was fed by ravens during a time of famine?
    Answer: Elijah.
14. Who lost all his possessions and yet praised God?
    Answer: Job.
15. Who wrote Psalm 23?
    Answer: David.
16. Who tried to overthrow his father and become king in
    his place?
    Answer: Absalom.
17. What people were thrown into a fiery furnace because
    they refused to worship an idol?
    Answer: Shadrach, Meshach, and Abednego.
18. Who was thrown into a den of lions because he
    refused to stop praying?
    Answer: Daniel.
19. Who was Peter's brother?
    Answer: Andrew.
20. Who came to see Jesus by night?
    Answer: Nicodemus.
21. Who denied Jesus?
    Answer: Peter.
22. Who betrayed Jesus?
    Answer: Judas.
23. Who anointed the feet of Jesus with precious oint-
    ment?
    Answer: Mary.
24. Who washed the disciples' feet?
    Answer: Jesus.
25. Who was let over a wall in a basket to escape his
    enemies?
    Answer: Paul.

Bible Drills

Divide into teams for maximum interest. Each person
on a team must find the verse before the first one can
stand up, read it, and be counted the winner. Make up
your own Bible drills by looking up in your Bible concordance topics such as: obedience, trust, faith, hope, joy,

light,heaven,oranyothersubjectyoumaybestudying.
Here'sonetogowiththedevotionalidea"WhatAbout
theFuture?"

The Future

Deuteronomy 5:29	1 Timothy 6:14
Deuteronomy 32:29	2 Timothy 4:8
Psalm 73:24	Titus 2:13
Isaiah 35:10	Hebrews 9:28
Isaiah 46:4	Hebrews 12:28
Jeremiah 29:11	James 5:8
John 14:3	1 Peter 1:13
John 10:28	1 Peter 5:4
Romans 8:16-17	2 Peter 3:13
Romans 8:18	1 John 2:17
1 Corinthians 15:51-52	1 John 3:1
2 Corinthians 5:1	Jude 24
Ephesians 2:7	Revelation 3:5
Philippians 3:20	Revelation 3:11
Colossians 3:4	Revelation 21:4
1 Thessalonians 4:16-17	Revelation 22:5

Paper and Pencil Games

Teens may work separately or in teams on these games.

WHICH BIBLE FATHER . . . ?

1. Honored his sons above the Lord? (1 Samuel 2:29)
2. Took an eleven-month boat trip with his three sons? (Genesis 7-8)
3. At God's command, consented to kill his own son? (Genesis 22)
4. Refused to be comforted when he believed his son to be dead? (Genesis 37:35)
5. Preferred one of his sons above the other? (Genesis 25:28)
6. Had two sons while exiled in a foreign land? (Genesis 41:51- 52)
7. Had a son who attempted to overthrow him as king? (2 Samuel 15)

8. Had two sons who became Jesus' disciples? (Matthew 4:21)
9. Fathered the forerunner of Jesus? (Luke 1)

Answers: 1. Eli, 2. Noah, 3. Abraham, 4. Jacob, 5. Isaac, 6. Joseph, 7. David, 8. Zebedee, 9. Zacharias

Add the word *some* to the clue. The first one is done for you.

1. Nice but not necessary—(handsome)
2. Some TV programs
3. Friendly arrangement
4. Scary
5. Kids who brag
6. What a Christian shouldn't be
7. What bad habits are
8. What a true Christian is
9. You're tempted to be this at home
10. When we especially need Jesus

Answers: 1. handsome, 2. gruesome, 3. twosome, 4. fearsome, 5. tiresome, 6. meddlesome, 7. worrisome, 8. winsome, 9. quarrelsome, 10. lonesome

Can you unscramble these words? The ones on the left are what football players do to help their team. The ones on the right are what Christians do at church on God's team.

Football Field	At Church
1. ntair-	1. moce-
2. npla-	2. chreap-
3. ssap-	3. cheta-
4. cktale-	4. yalp rogan-
5. nur-	5. nclea-
6. tnup-	6. rushe-
7. ckik-	7. pleh-
8. abll rryac-	8. viteni-
9. choac-	9. gisn-

10. kclob-   10. sliten-

Answers: 1. train, 2. plan, 3. pass, 4. tackle, 5. run, 6. punt, 7. kick, 8. carry ball, 9. coach, 10. block

1. come, 2. preach, 3. teach, 4. play organ, 5. clean, 6. usher, 7. help, 8. invite, 9. sing, 10. listen

A CHOICE CHOICE

Fill in the blanks with letters to show what you may choose to have a good life now and forever. Use the King James Version or the *New American Standard Bible* to find the word if you get stuck.

C _ _ _ _ _ _   (A person—Romans 5:6)
H _ _ _ _ _   (A place—Matthew 5:3)
O _ _ _ _ _ _ _ _   (A way of life—Romans 1:5)
I _ _ _ _ _ _ _ _ _ _ _   (Teaching—Proverbs 8:10)
C _ _ _ _ _ _ _ _   (Companions—Proverbs
  _ _ _ _ _ _ _ _   1:10)
E _ _ _ _ _ _ _ _ _ _   (Exciting reward—John
                             10:28)

Answers: Christ, Heaven, Obedience, Instruction, Christian Friends, Eternal Life

PRAYING MAZO

Divide into twos. See who can finish first.

Can you find and circle in the puzzle the following words about praying? They go across and down.

```
K G I V E T H A N K S Z      Alone
E V E R Y W H E R E O P      Always
E Y W C A D F A L O N E      Anytime
P R A I S E J N R T S Q      Ask
O K M R K O A Y X L P E      Everywhere
N W E F O R O T H E R S      For me
B W I T H F A I T H S N      For others
R I P L F O R M E E S U      Give thanks
U T O G E T H E R H A M      Keep on
A L W A Y S Y X O P W R      Praise
                             Together
                             With faith
```

"Teamwork Scramble" and "Praying Mazo" were printed

in *Action* (Winona Lake, Ind.: Light and Life Press). Used by permission.

WHO MET CHRIST . . . ?

Divide into twos or larger teams. Youth can do this matching quiz from memory or look up the corresponding Scriptures, if necessary:

1. Riding in a chariot	Genesis 28:10-22—Jacob
2. In a tree	1 Samuel 3:1-10—Samuel
3. By a roadside begging	Mark 10:46-52—Bartimaeus
4. In bed	Luke 19:45—Zaccheus
5. At his mother's knee	John 4:6-7—Woman of Samaria
6. On the road to Damascus	Acts 8:26-38—Ethiopian eunuch
7. By a well	Acts 9:1-6—Saul (Paul)
8. In jail	Acts 16:9—Philippian jailer
9. At the bottom of a ladder	Acts 16:13-14—Lydia
10. At a riverside prayer meeting	2 Timothy 3:14-15—Timothy

Answers: 1. Ethiopian eunuch, 2. Zaccheus, 3. Bartimaeus, 4. Samuel, 5. Timothy, 6. Saul (Paul), 7. Woman of Samaria, 8. Philippian jailer, 9. Jacob, 10. Lydia
Note: You will need to make copies of these paper and pencil games.

8
Crafty Activities

A good way to develop abilities, have fun, and save money is to make and do many of your own crafts, decorations, and visual aids. So let's get crafty in our activities!

Crafts

There are many booklets available with detailed instructions on how to do various crafts. Crafts for crafts' sake alone are not for you as a teacher, except when you're planning a craft sale to earn money for a service project. Instead, you will only do arts and crafts that add to or enhance your teaching and learning experiences. The few described here will help with program plans mentioned in this book. Consult craft manuals for help with other craft activities.

BUILD A BIBLE TOWN

To help your junior highers become acquainted with the books of the Bible, make a Bible Town together. One small group can work on Old Town (Old Testament) and another on New Town (New Testament).

Streets of Old Town should be named according to the

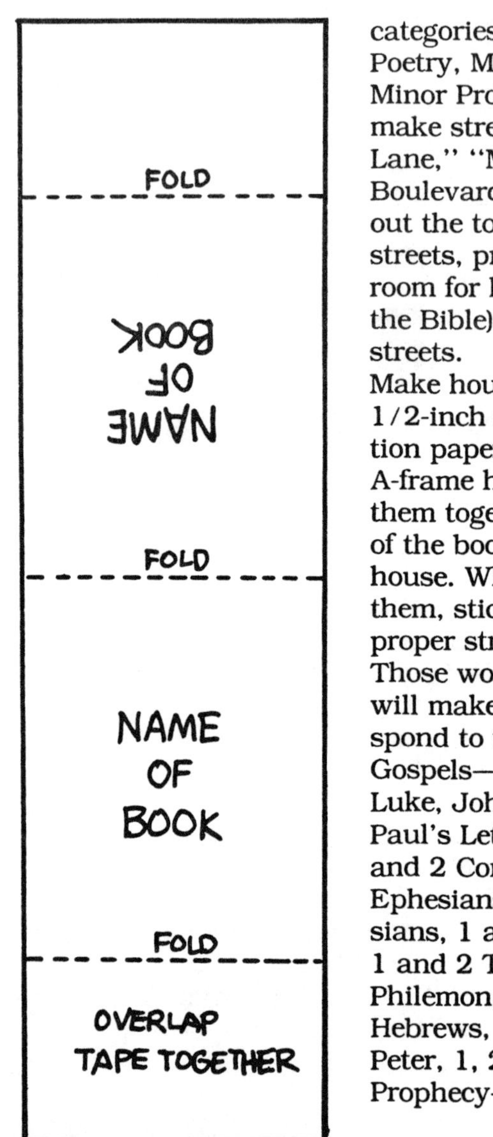

categories: Moses, History, Poetry, Major Prophets, and Minor Prophets. Let the youth make street signs: "Poetry Lane," "Major Prophets Boulevard," and so on. Lay out the town with these five streets, providing enough room for houses (the books of the Bible) to be placed on the streets.

Make houses of 6-inch by 1 1/2-inch strips of construction paper. Fold to make an A-frame house. Before taping them together, print the name of the book of the Bible on the house. When you have taped them, stick them on the proper streets.

Those working on New Town will make streets to correspond to those categories: Gospels—Matthew, Mark, Luke, John; History—Acts; Paul's Letters—Romans, 1 and 2 Corinthians, Galatians, Ephesians, Philippians, Colossians, 1 and 2 Thessalonians, 1 and 2 Timothy, Titus, Philemon; General Letters— Hebrews, James, 1 and 2 Peter, 1, 2, and 3 John, Jude; Prophecy—Revelation.

BUILD A BIBLE BOOKSHELF

Does someone have an old bookcase you could use? Have the kids cover old books (you can get them for almost nothing at garage sales) with butcher paper, printing on the spine of each book the name of a book of the Bible. Mix up the books in the case and let groups of four see how quickly they can rearrange them correctly.

SHAPE CHRISTMAS GOODIE
CANDLES

Collect from youth and other church members the following throw-away items: paper towel tubes, foil pot pie tins, and heavy cardboard paper tablet backs. You will need one of each for each candle.

Cut the tablet backs into 6-inch diameter circles for the "saucer." Tempera paint the circles, or glue a 6-inch circle of pretty Christmas paper on them. Or, for simplicity, merely use a foil pot pie tin for the candle saucer or bowl.

Cover the tubes with shiny solid-colored gift-wrapping paper. Tape these upright, one candle on each saucer circle or pie tin.

For the "flame," cut strips of red or silver foil, 5 inches long by 4 1/2 inches deep. Glue these inside the top of the candle, lapping the long ends over each other.

Fill the tube candle with small cookies and candies, baked by the junior highers. Fill some specially marked candles with dietetic goodies for diabetics.

Twist the foil into a flame-like shape to complete the closed Christmas goodie candle.

Take your "made with love" candles to elderly people or children confined in homes or hospitals. Stay in each room long enough to vocalize your love.

CONSTRUCT A "TWELVE DAYS OF CHRISTMAS" GIFT BOX

This item is a container that teens fill with twelve small gifts to be enjoyed (one a day) during a person's extended stay in the hospital during the holiday season.

Collect from young people and other church members a number of sturdy boxes with removable lids. These boxes must be large enough to hold a dozen small gifts. If some bring in small boxes, these may be used to hold some small gifts to be included in the larger boxes.

Meet together to cover the boxes and lids separately with colorful gift-wrapping paper. Wrap homemade and purchased gifts and place them in the big covered box. Attach a jaunty bow on the box and go gift-giving. Tell each recipient that the plan is to open one gift each day to add daily cheer to the hospital stay.

What would be appropriate to put in the box? Items would vary, according to the age and sex of the one to receive the box, of course. Some items should carry a spiritual message, although others could be just for fun. Stationery or note cards, a small New Testament (for readers), a puzzle, paper and pencil games, a simple toy, a small bottle of cologne or powder, a book, a bookmark, a Christmas table decoration, and a silk pillow corsage would be suitable gifts.

For each box, prepare a picture puzzle of the youth group. Have a photo "bug" take a picture of the kids. Enlarge this photo into as many pictures as boxes planned. Write the names of the youth, in the order in which they appear, at the bottom of a cardboard square, sized so the puzzle can be assembled upon it. Cut the photo into puzzle shapes (few pieces for a child—more for a teen or adult), and put the pieces and the cardboard into a sealable plastic bag.

Attractive stand-up nativity table-top scenes are easily made from cut-out figures of discarded Christmas cards. These can be arranged as simple dioramas in boxes or oval-shaped metal tins. Canned fish containers make nice "housing" for homemade manger scenes.

Decorations

Young people will enjoy decorating for parties and specialized meetings. Creativity will bud and bloom as it is encouraged and used. Give youth a few suggestions and let them go with a theme.

MAKE MAY DAY MAGIC

Magnify spring with a blooming potted plant on each table at your May Day Tea or Salad Luncheon. Geraniums look like spring personified when "dressed" in pastel gingham.

Choose lime, yellow, and pink small-checkered cloth. To

"dress" a 4-inch pot, use pinking shears to cut a circle 12 inches in diameter for each pot. Pleat it in place with your hands. Glue the pleats in place with tiny dots of clear-drying glue. Tie a perky bow of a matching solid-color ribbon around the center of the pot. Place the plant on a table covered with a solid-colored cloth the same color as the plant's ribbon.

If your theme is developed into a dinner, use your gingham scraps to make matching May Basket nut cups. With pinking shears, cut circles 5 inches in diameter for each 2-inch nut cup. Pleat the cloth up around the cups and complete them as you did the pots. Glue a chenille stick handle on each cup. Use assorted colored nut cups on each table.

For a buffet, make larger matching May Baskets to hang on a painted potted branch or mug tree. Use souffle cups for these bigger baskets, making the "dress" circle three inches larger in diameter than the diameter of the souffle cup. You can put silk flowers or additional candies in these May Baskets.

POP A PIÑATA

Breaking the piñata (pronounced pin yá ta), a decorated pottery jar filled with goodies, is an exciting part of a Mexican festivity.

You may have a clay pot you want to sacrifice at the party. But it's cheaper and more fun for a group to make a piñata out of paper maché with a balloon.

If you have a large junior high group, divide into several teams and have a piñata making contest. Three or four could work well on each piñata. It's a bit messy, but making this colorful decoration is almost as much fun as breaking it.

1. Decide what bird or animal you want your piñata to be.
2. Blow up and tie a large round balloon for the body. Use smaller round balloons and long ones for the head and legs. Tape the balloon body together.

3. Tear newspapers into 1-inch strips of varying lengths.
   Put them in a box. You'll need lots.
4. Mix flour and water paste, using equal amounts of
   flour and water. If a thinner paste is desired, add
   more water.
5. Cover the balloons with strips of newspaper dipped
   into the paste. To remove excess paste, run the strip
   lightly through the middle finger, forefinger, and
   thumb.
6. Fasten a string loop on the top of the form, keeping
   the loop open. Continue applying strips of newspaper
   all over the balloons until all have been covered with
   at least two layers.
7. Form ears, feet, and other features with additional
   builds of paste-wet strips.
8. Dry your piñata for a day or two.
9. Paint the piñata with tempera paints or water colors.
   A tissue paper tail, wings, or a mane may be glued
   on to complete the bird or animal.
10. When it is dry, cut a small hole in the top of the
    piñata. This will burst the body balloon. Drop cov-
    ered candies and nuts into the cavity. Cover the hole
    with tape or a layer of tissue paper.
11. On the day of the party, pull a rope through the loop
    on the top of the piñata and hang it from the ceiling
    about 2 feet higher than the heads of the young
    people.
12. Blindfold youths to take turns striking at the piñata
    with a stick, trying to burst it to release the goodies.

Pop! Splat! Scramble for the sweets!!

LIGHT UP THE PATHWAY

For an outdoor party, light the pathway with luminaries. Put 3 or 4 inches of sand or rocks in a number of
paper sacks. Stand a candle up in the middle of each one.
Line the pathway with the filled sacks. Light the candles
just before party-time. The sacks will prevent the wind
from blowing out the candles. These luminaries cast a
nice glow on the scene.

CREATE A FLAMING VOLCANO

Add realism to a luau (Hawaiian feast) with a flaming
volcano.

On a platter, form a volcanic mountain of crushed ice.
Hollow a small crater in the top, just big enough for a bottle cap to rest in. Keep your volcano in the freezer until
party time. Take it out, put Easter grass on the platter,
and fill the bottle cap with lemon extract.

Strike a match to the extract. Your flaming volcano will
grace the table of delightful Hawaiian edibles.

Visual Aids

Maintain interest and increase learning by using an
ever-changing variety of visual aids. Films and filmstrips
are great, but are not always accessible or affordable.
Young people will enjoy making visuals and will learn
while creating them.

SEW UP SOME BYKOTA

Hem by hand or machine the top, bottom, and end
edges of a strip of solid color material, 3-inches wide by
12- to 14-inches long (depending on arm size). Print
BYKOTA on the armband with crayons. Place the band
on folded newspaper, lay a sheet of tissue paper over the
crayoned word, and press with a warm iron. Fasten the
armband with iron-on velcro.

MAKE YOUR OWN INVITATIONS

Go creative with invitations to parties. Cut them into
shapes that relate to the party theme. Save postage by
delivering by hand all you can. Mail out only the ones
you can't reach by foot, bike, or car. A written invitation
reinforced with a verbal encouragement ("We want you to
come") is hard to refuse.

The pineapple pattern would be appropriate for a luau.
A fall leaf could invite "hobos" to drop in to Hobo Hollow.

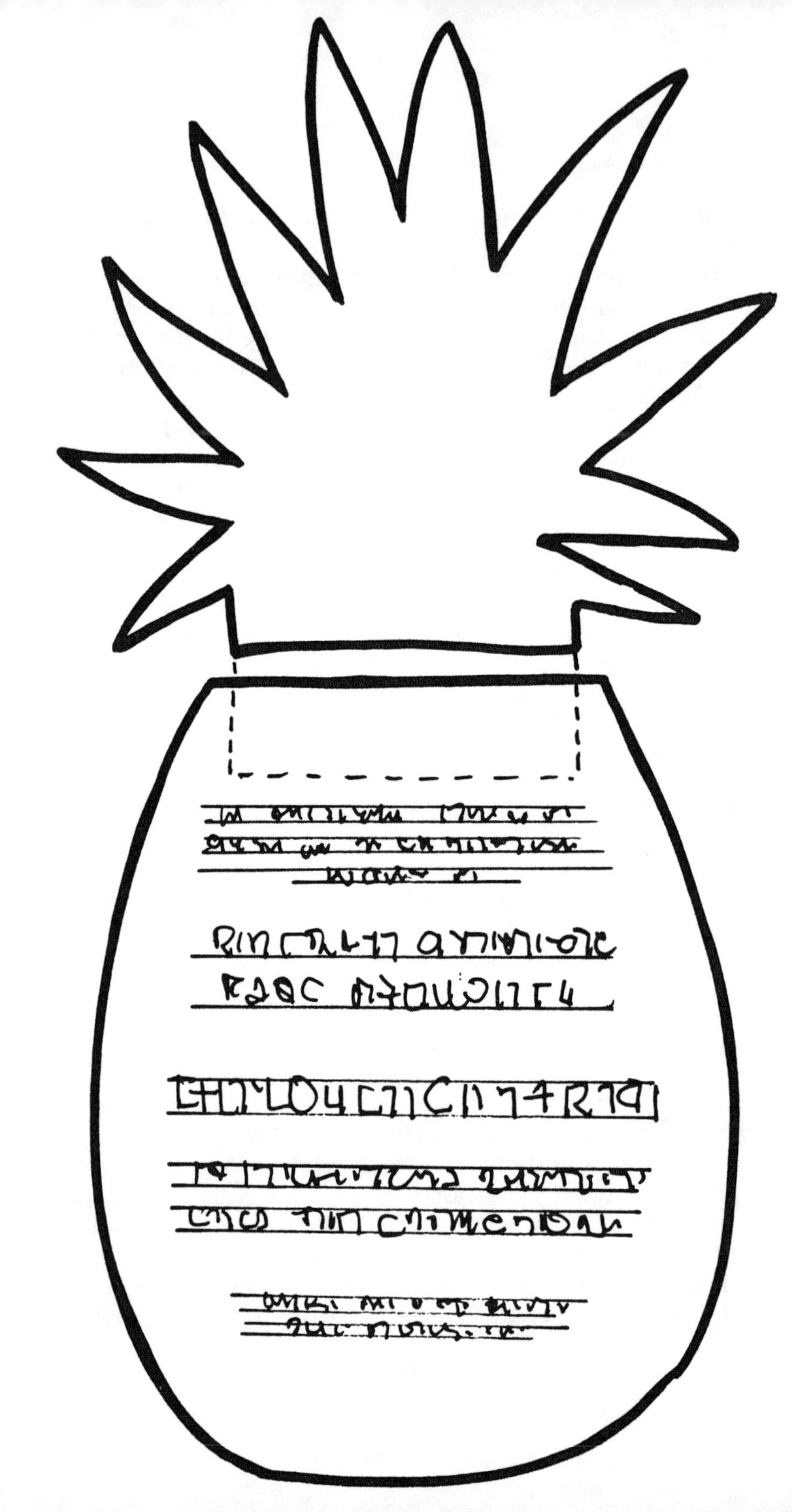

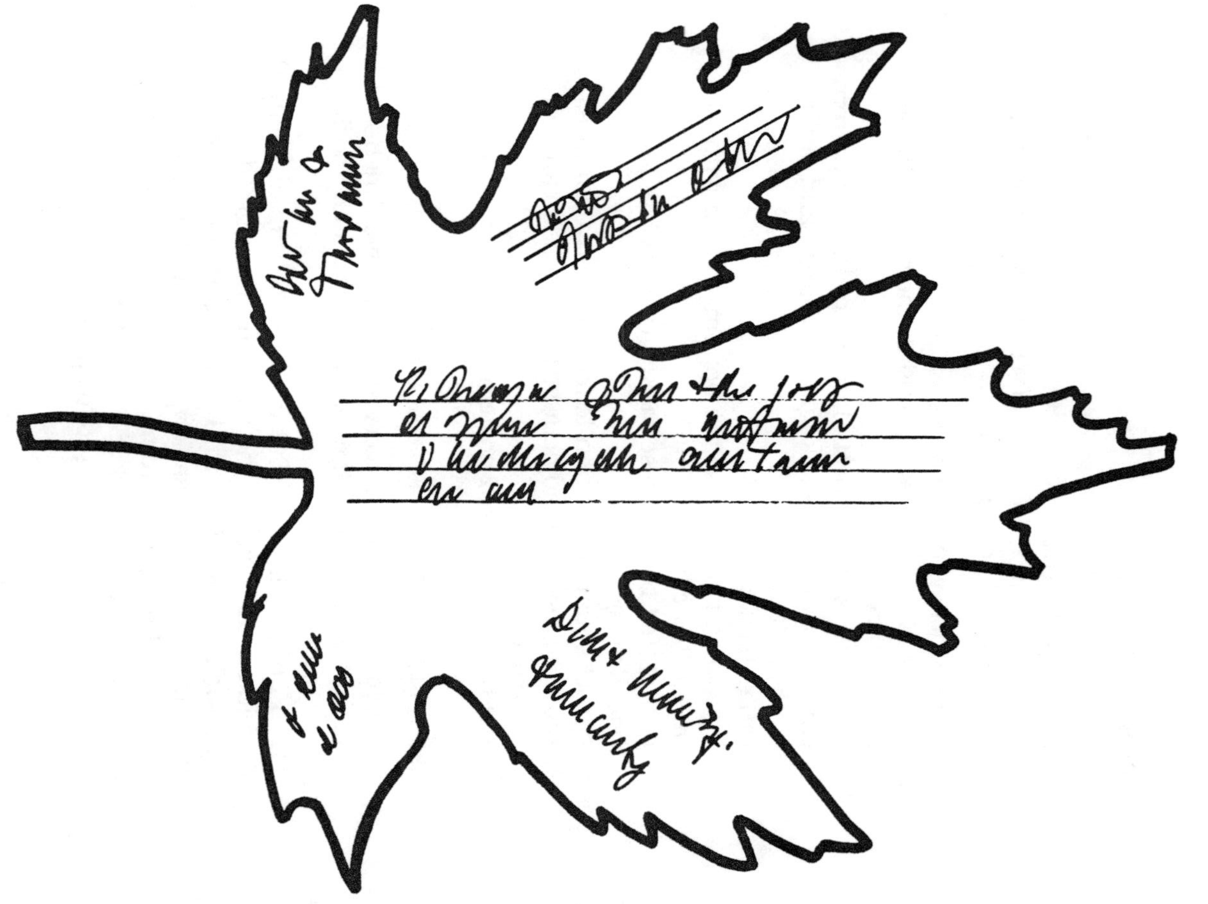

Print up lots of posters to reinforce learning experiences. Try the lapped letter.

Poster board isn't cheap, so try these economy measures. Paste your messages on:

1. newspaper want ad sheets
2. newsprint left over at the end of the roll at the newspaper office
3. wallpaper sample sheets from discontinued patterns
4. cardboard used in packaging stockings and other clothing items
5. tablet backs
6. lightweight boxes (use the bottom and lid with sides on for 3-D effect)
7. corrugated boxes (these make great textured backdrops)
8. carpet squares (stick on letters with straight pins)
9. box dividers for ready-cut strips for flash cards or sentence strips
10 the backside of used posters

MAKE A REUSABLE STRIP FOLDER CHART

Recycle an ordinary grocery sack into two functional strip folder charts. Give the extra one to a neighboring teacher or group.

Open up the big sack. Cut from the bottom up along the side fold on each side of the sack and through the middle of the sack bottom. Fold in the sides and down the bottom. The bottom of the sack will become the top of your strip chart. Fold pleats from left to right at desired intervals to form shallow pockets. Staple, sew, or tape the left and right edges of the bag to keep the folds in place.

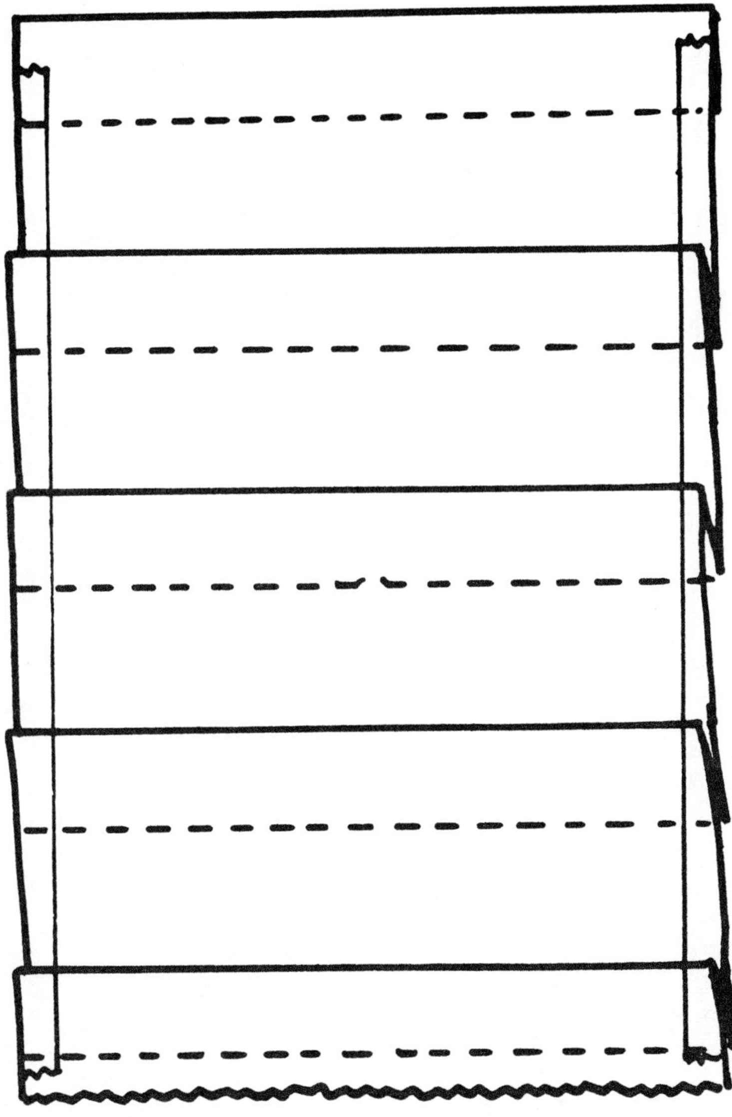

Any size bag can be used. Small ones work well with small groups; big ones are better for messages to be read from a distance.

Did these few simple ideas get your creativity flowing? Let it flow on into more and more crafty activities!

9
On Your Own

Some bleak day you may have no printed program ideas available that fit the needs of your particular youth group. You are on your own. This chapter may help relieve your anxiety.

First, pray for God's guidance. Now decide specifically what your teens need a lesson on. Your program content will be teachings and activities designed to meet that particular need. Include only plans relevant to your determined need. "Rabbits" (distractions and tangents) that try to hop in must be chased elsewhere, or, if persistent, perhaps developed into another program for a later date.

The selected need will suggest your theme or topic. Determine to teach more than facts. Teach to change lives for the Lord.

Now that you have a theme, look up your theme word in the dictionary, a Bible concordance, and your hymnbook index. The dictionary, besides clarifying your understanding of the theme word, may suggest related words you should run reference on.

List all references and songs that mention your theme word and its relatives. Next, read carefully every Bible verse and every hymn on your topic. Discard any that do not directly relate to your subject. Read the remaining Bible verses in several translations and paraphrases. Words may vary enough that a youth might not find what you point out in his particular Bible. The prepared teacher will then be alerted to handle "that's not what my Bible says" negative notes and point out agreements in the Word.

Consult a commentary and a Bible scholar in your church, if you aren't secure in your knowledge of the Bible lesson you have chosen. Outline the material, so that you lead to an application of biblical truth to today's needs.

Search for current events that relate to your theme. Avoid a story for story's sake, but a contemporary issue makes a great introduction and/or conclusion to a youth program.

Plan a variety of methods for learning. Again, activity for activity's sake is a "no-no," but a meaningful, correlated activity opens another "gate," besides the ear-gate, to learning. Besides, busy hands don't poke the neighbor or stick gum under the table.

Hymns can beautifully set the mood and introduce or conclude a program. They may be sung, read as poetry, or spoken as a speech choir, using selected verses or the whole song.

Some songs have such a marvelous biblical message that you may, on occasion, build an entire program around a song or several related ones.

Study the song stanza by stanza in groups or as a whole. Does the song contain Bible references? Some hymnbooks identify these biblical references. If so, look up the Scripture passage. Does the song agree with the Bible? Decide on the theme of the song and each stanza.

Determine what effect this song should have on the life of a teen today—on your teens specifically. Would singing this song improve anyone's day?

Focus on the biblical injunction in Ephesians 5:19, "Speaking to one another in psalms and hymns and spiritual songs, singing and making melody with your heart to the Lord." What we sing *does* make a difference in how our day goes. It would be a "PTL" indeed, if your musical program helped your teens to glorify God daily instead of the devil with their music.

In developing this "on your own" program, plan more material than you think you can cover. But decide what you can omit if time runs out. Remember, the introduction and the application are the most important parts of your program. The introduction catches their attention and leads them to learn. The application is the need-meeting part of your program. If you must cut somewhere, cut in the middle.

If kids get you off the subject, work with the new idea awhile and promise to get back to it with the individual concerned—or the group, if the interest is widespread. Then get back to your plan.

Keep your promise. Perhaps the sidetrack issue should be your next program, brought to your teens "by popular demand."

Some possible themes to consider for January through December are suggested here. Those marked with an asterisk (*) indicate that a devotional on this topic is included in chapter 3 of this book. These printed thoughts could help you in developing your own personalized program.

Themes

January

      Journey into a New Year
      New Beginnings
      Goals*
      New Year's Musings*

February

      The Greatest Is Love
      BYKOTA*
      Story of Saint Valentine
      Love and Marriage*

March

      Forward March!

Story of Saint Patrick (foreign missions)
Everyone Bring One (build up your youth group)
Service Projects*

April

New Life!
What the Resurrection Means to Us
Let It Rain (How God uses trouble in our lives)

May

Home, Sweet Home
Home Is Where the Hassle Is*
Mother's Day (something special for Mom)

June

Vacation from What?
Banish Boredom with Service Projects*
Father's Day (something special for Dad)

July

Patriotism Is for Christians
Fun in the Sun (picnics, volleyball, beach parties)
Plan an Outreach Program

August

Outdoor Activities (campfires, lake sing)
Camping
Nature Studies

September

Back to School
The Harvest (it *does* matter how you act!)
What Difference Does the Bible Make?*

October

What Do You Know About Halloween?
Danger of Occult (explore superstitions, rock music)
Reformation: Story of Martin Luther

November

Attitude of Gratitude*
Helping the Hungry*

How the Pilgrims Did It

December

Christmas Is Giving*
Origin of Christmas Tradition
Prophecies of the Coming of Christ

You are now *on your own.* But—are you? No, not really. Check out God's promises to you as you disciple your young people. Do your homework in God's Word. The following verses offer precious promises of God's working with you, giving you guidance and confidence: Matthew 10:17-20; Matthew 18:20; Matthew 28:18-20; Acts 18:10.

10

Operation on Target

Teaching junior highers is a challenge, admittedly. Mission impossible? No, never! The Lord who called you to the task says, "The things impossible with men are possible with God" (Luke 18:27).

He encourages you to remember,

> "For My thoughts are not your thoughts, neither are your ways My ways," declares the Lord. "For as the rain and the snow come down from heaven, and do not return there without watering the earth, and making it bear and sprout, and furnishing seed to the sower and bread to the eater; so shall My word be which goes forth from My mouth; it shall not return to Me empty without accomplishing what I desire, and without succeeding in the matter for which I sent it." [Isaiah 55:8-11]

Ask wisdom of Him in meeting the spiritual needs of your youth (James 1:5). Feed them upon God's Word.

Above all, love them. "But now abide faith, hope, love, these three; but the greatest of these is love" (1 Corinthians 13:13).

Don't keep the faith. Give it away to your junior

highers. "Cast your bread on the surface of the waters, for you will find it after many days" (Ecclesiastes 11:1). Don't be discouraged if you don't see immediate results. Sow the seed faithfully, water it with your prayers, and trust God to give the increase.

Your mission will be accomplished. *You will operate on target.*

God bless you and yours!

NOTES

NOTES

NOTES

NOTES

NOTES

NOTES

NOTES

NOTES

NOTES